Paavithratha

The Purity - A Book on Life's Attributes

notionpress
.com

Paavithratha

The Purity - A Book on Life's Attributes

A M Nagesh

notionpress
.com

Notion Press

Old No. 38, New No. 6

McNichols Road, Chetpet

Chennai - 600 031

First Published by Notion Press 2016

ISBN 978-93-5206-865-4

Disclaimer

I am not a pundit. I humbly suggest that all my verbs, adjectives, nouns, idioms and phrases illustrating the world of Vedic literature are conjectural; this work is based on my experiences.

Dedicated to

All Teachers

Man obliged his entire life to acquire knowledge,

Man did not try to find out what knowledge is all about

Man used his time for

Knowing the learnt knowledge.

Man never attained liberation because of his forgone focusing skill.

PARIVARTHANA - the change

PAAVITHRATHA

NEURO PSYCHO SPIRITUALISM -Swim Lane Reppresentation

Me	AGO BRAHMAN (Infinite Cosmos)	YOGA (at its true perspective)	HUMAN (the forgotten humanity)		
Mine	OPEN MEDITATION (my invention)	AURA (the SWAMIJI'S possess)	WIFE AND WI-FI (to compare)	MY DOUBLE FIST FORE HAND SHOT (a change would mean more)	
Society	THE KUTEERA (sacred school)	VEDHA (not VADHE the SAMHARA or to kill)	KUMBH (the mind full)		
My Actions/Practice	THE CONFESSIONS- NOT TO REMEMBER (to meditate on)	THU THU MEI MEI (the malicious)	BETTING and GAMBLING (in relevance to SAMUDRA MANTHANA)	ORAL FIXER'S (to remember the Freud)	ADDICTION (finding truth on its definition)
Corporate-Institutional	PATHANJALI MAHARUSHI (the Grand Father of Psychiatry)	LANGUAGE (to remember the philosopher's)			
World/Universe	SAMUDRA MANTHANA (the churning of the 'mind ocean')	COSMOS (the orderly)	PRALAYA (at a distant time)		
Beyond/Above me/Almighty	YAMA DHARMARAJA (the Lord of Hell)				
Conceit(practicable)	GATE THEORY (the art of MASSAGE)	LANGUAGE BUSTERS (the boastfulness)	IMPOTENCY VS TELEPOTENCY (potent the common word)	SHIVA'S TRILOGY (the THRISHUUL)	ARITHMETIC AND DOGMATIC (the job compared to numbers)
Abstract	DANCE OF THE DEMOCRACY v/s DANCE AT THE STADIUM (comparison)	COLOUR TERRORISM (no remedy in near feature)	SOCIAL ATOM BOMB (a word SADHBHAVANA to meditate on)	WALKING DEAD (man's true nature)	SUSPENDED PARTICLES (to ponder on)
Reckoner-Referencial	BRAIN-Madhva,Ramanuja & Shankara (the interpretations are pertaining to the BRAINS connectivity)	GARUDA KAMBA (the temple pillar)	THREE MUSKETEERS OF DEATH (Athos, Aramis, Prothos and NACHIKETHA)		
Metric-Mensurational	CRIMINAL INDEX (an index much needed)				

PRARTHANA - the prayers
(the book on OPEN MEDITATION)

Contents

PREFACE

I strongly believe that hobbies are a fillip to increase man's self-esteem for positive life adaptation. I intend to delve into the duality existing between the individual's professional *(Vritthi)* career and their hobby. A hobbyist (*Pravritthi)* has a positive approach to life because of their individualistic innate art, which when applied in the society helps to decrease boredom. This innate art is not included for the study if it is his profession; such knowledge has two useful dimensions when compared to professional knowledge. The knowledge-based hobbies could possess self-healing powers and could also bring happiness to others, for example, pleasing people from displaying various arts possessed by artists.

A profession provides a distinct, comfortable path, which is a basic necessity for living. However, this path is materialistic, and cannot provide happiness. Hobbies, philanthropy and music provide the crucial mysticism that is required in the present-day hollow, unsafe and hocus-pocus world. I strongly feel that it is neither my profession nor my medical prescription that helped my depressed patients, but the virtues and values I learnt from my hobbies and experience that did wonders to the patients' health. A doctor should not always be in the same role. As he gains experience, he should don the role of a teacher. The term 'doctor' is a Latin word for teacher. This knowledge I have acquired through my literary works. I took up learning as a hobby. The wisdom I acquired by this hobby (virtues and values learnt from reading the Upanishath and Puranas) helped to relieve patients' anxiety by counselling. Probably, this results in an upbeat mood of the depressed patients when they come for my psychiatric treatment. It is well known that the number of depressed a psychiatrist sees in his clinic or hospital is just a tip of the iceberg. Hence, we can conclude that the society is overburdened with depressive people. Personally, I feel that the reason for this prevailing depression could be because 'the world is against hedonism.' In the pursuit of providing happiness to an ever-changing psycho-socio-economical fabric of this society, each individual with his diversified dual knowledge, learnt and innate, is trying to provide the best part of his professional hobby skills to the society. This would help to keep up the tempo in spreading happiness. In these epistemic ventures, a scientist endeavours to infer those inferences on happiness in the society, and in doing so, he is in competition with others, and thus, this leads to anxiety. Hence, when he is professionally anxious, his innate hobby skills keep a check on his own irrational anxiety.

I can draw an analogy to the above-mentioned illness. When I was diagnosed with adenocarcinoma of the rectum, for which I underwent a radical surgery with a permanent colostomy on my abdomen, my profession could not pacify my depression. It was my innate interesting sports that helped me regain my happiness. After I boldly overcame my illness, people praised me by saying, "Gods must have showered mercy on you, it is all because of your friends' wishes." They also attributed my improvement to my strong will. There are many similar cock and bull stories. I believe that it was my sports hobby that paved the way for better prognosis. This was possible because of my team of doctors who performed exhaustive alterations in my body and also by the esoteric chemicals that administered to my body, I am ever grateful to them.

In relation to the aspect of profession and hobby, a philosopher venturing to explore metaphysics is constantly snubbed, argued, criticised and persecuted. This had resulted in constant fear; the innate sense of self-belief on their expounded treatise has provided enough or enormous material for our brains to think on our origin, our living and finally our decay. Their extraordinary and future visionary ideas have enhanced our thinking process while we try to understand this universe. By adopting their literature and after their careful scrutiny, it might help us in understanding life better; applying their philosophy to life would make us better humans, and after sharing these thoughts in the society, it would always result in more happiness and smiles.

When an intellectual is restrained in an asylum, he might think of ending his life. He could prefer death rather than the absence of physical freedom. As days passed, he perceived his death was closer and found himself happier for the silence he had developed. In this silence, he could have got enlightened as to his part in this universe, would have gone into the greater depths of cosmic wonders, and would have had thoughts of enjoyment. Once again, he had found happiness after losing his earlier depression and felt more privileged to end his life, as he was ready to unite with the Lord. At this phase of life, he called all his admirers, comprising his followers and non-followers, inside the asylum where he was chained. He addressed the gathered people as "Grievers and non-grievers, my day has approached to pass on my intellectual wealth.

Message-bearers (a person bearing a good message to another) and non-bearers, we have approached the day where my depression and delusion have disappeared. Believers and non-believers, the day has approached wherein in silence I found the Lord, to whom I am forever indebted. The day has approached where I solemnize to leave, to understand the 'know nothings' to 'know everything's', in the quest for the soul's happiness. If my literary sentiments are passed on, passed on forever from this day of my death, I am a liberated man." This was similar to the journey of Lord Buddha, except that he did not commit suicide. This intellectual was a step ahead of Lord Buddha to reach the infinite, whereas Lord Buddha did so in silence. Lord Buddha's equation was simple. His life's equation was one word, *Achintha* or *A-shoka* (no worry). Today, I think Lord Buddha could have arrived at this equation on a proponent "Open meditation."

Two thousand and five hundred years ago, Socrates was indifferent to the then Greek culture, as he did not accept money for his teachings. He never took credit for the introduction of new concepts in his 'teachings.' The reason was that he never considered to have taught anyone. This philosophy of Socrates was contrary to the teachings of Tao, where the Tao preachers believe only in teaching and not in the philosophy. Socrates possessed a strong belief of Sophists, and he had promulgated that "philosophy is from heaven." He firmly believed that only education could alter the youths' future. He was a person with a peculiar personality, as he never wrote his teachings. His followers, just like the *Boddhi Tatwas*, wrote all his doctrines. These '*Boddhi Tatwas*' were accepted, written and nurtured by Buddha's followers. Socrates viewed life in a different perspective, similar to Buddha or as per our Hindu philosophy. *Socrates* had preached his philosophy by explaining the means and methods to live. He was the one who gave credit to the art of inquiry and for adding and deducing in the field of one's own consciousness. To my knowledge, he was not a good teacher but had motivated the intelligent youth and he used to assign them a particular task. His students deduced the task. Meanwhile, Socrates asked them to explain elaborately the same. He was ironical towards his students, and he did not call them as his students, instead he called them as his partners. What a great quality he had possessed! He was known for his intellect. He told people that he listened to God's voices and that God had asked him to do only "Good." He held the opinion that art could be taught but not virtues. We should learn virtues on our own and they are present only in a liberated mind. According to Socrates, the virtues can be harnessed by self and is also related to the 'gene' unlike art, which can only be taught. Hence, he had more attachment to goodness. For all of Socrates's good virtues, he was charged with sedition, impiety and of corrupting the young minds. What an irony in this world of tyranny where good is locked and the bad is circulated all over the world.

A spiritualist is also a person who brings peace and happiness to people. However, his hobby never permitted him to become a Buddha. A spiritualist learnings made him a modern King, and this could be the probable reason for not being able to free himself from his obsessive euphoria. Professionally, spiritualists are fine but they habitually treat happiness as a merchandise. This is also true with many professionals. Imagine or meditate that if an individual's world of ignorant obsessions becomes topsy-turvy, he acquires the required knowledge to enable him to straighten out the same world table, so that this tilted table now holds the cups and plates filled with joy; then feel what would happen to this society? This brings more cheer. If the previously mentioned tilt does happen to me, I call the same phenomenon as *Santhrupthi* (contentment, or in Kannada it is otherwise called as *Nemmadi*) rather than claiming to have achieved total happiness.

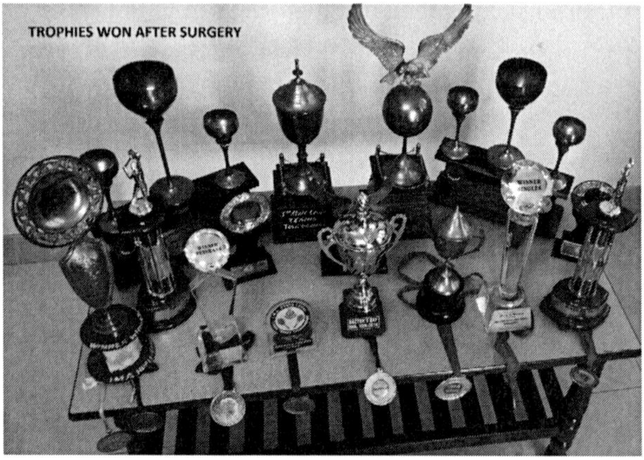

INTRODUCTION

When the world became fast-paced, a new trend emerged. Man walked around in a trendy attire but was only elegant on the outside, with being shattered internally. The frustrations in him found no vent, and he was left with no other choice but to keep accumulating worries and to have bouts of severe brooding regarding the past. In this previously mentioned fury, man failed to bring about a suitable remedy. The man hoped science would deliver him of his unhappiness. The reason for this scenario could be because the role of God is dwindling rapidly. In the past, 'science' was meant to be a difficult proposition. In this confusion, man, during his evolutionary period, tried to find a meaning to his own self-created anarchy, in which he succeeded partially. He christened his meaning as the "solace."

When the evolved man reasoned deeply, his happiness was more materialistic rather than the psychological. Hence, bliss was a farfetched concept. Therefore, in this mundane world, the word 'solace' is providential and self-researched by the evolved man. 'solace' is neither heroin that can be synthesised in the laboratories nor can it be harvested in the fields; solace is there for our discovery only in the micro cosmos or the *Nano Brahman*. The self-researched solace is a penance to man's fickle mind. The determined, modern man was crushed and snubbed by the rational, refined past medieval thoughts; thus evolved a simple and humble man of today. I presume to find a glee on the reader's face when he focuses on my statement and his cognizance thinks about a better approval. I want to express serious thoughts to resist their glee and to have their focused attention to be able to prune the ill twigs of life for a better yield of goodness later. I do not want my readers to be disinterested as in the Second World War, in which women seeked the pleasure of clients, as they had lost their spouses in the war zone, which led to sexual fidelity and thriving of slush flesh markets. Forgive me for this statement, as these are not my thoughts but a talk by the then war historians. The present-day informative technologies and sciences have failed to provide meaningful theories to the future worries and also for the past ones. Well, to my knowledge, while explaining the solace in the present context, the new frontiers of science have failed to create paraphernalia, which could provide interaction and help to understand the sorrow of human in the present complicated society. If at all we have happiness, then I am sure that there could be many theories existing to explain it, but scientists fail to provide total happiness to mankind and also are incapable to provide answers to the mundane.

Today, the field of psychiatric armoury has new well designed, with least side effects producing, psychiatric drug molecules to treat depression. In actuality, these drugs have failed or are not able to provide happiness to man. Hence, the role of psychiatry intervention is been questioned. I am amazed to find innumerable anti-psychiatry websites when I searched for psychiatry websites on the internet. To my astonishment, I found only few stand-alone 'psychiatry' websites from the search engines of God-given Pandora box. Many erstwhile psychiatrists view that future psychiatry is toothless and lacks sharpness to provide required happiness while tackling mental depressions with antidepressant drugs. In today's scenario, the psychiatrists' talk on psychiatry appears as a myth. Psychiatry cannot answer all our various complicated lifestyles, different life behaviours we exhibit and also the innumerable life deficits we harbour. There is a question as to whether to believe or not. If so, then 'why' is that such question arises?

NEURO-PSYCHO SPIRITUALISM
(A New Subject)

My first interest towards psychiatry was biological. In my practice, I have found the present society actually play a greater role for diagnosis and the management of many psychiatric illnesses. The same was taught at my institute during my psychiatry diploma course; candidly, I had cared too little for their teachings. As days progressed, I felt my spiritual sense was best suited compared to all. Today we talk about multiple senses while understanding and treating psychiatry patients. How could this happen? To explain briefly, at a gym, we do isometric exercises to increase the volume of our deltoid muscle. Similarly, when we exercise our different brain structures by reading various ancient Vedanthic scriptures, probably this type of reading exercise would lead us to acquire more than five senses. These dimensions would help a treating psychiatrist to view many psychiatric diseases more emphatically and he could empathise with the mentally challenged patient in a better manner.

When I began reading *Pathanjali* dossiers, I got enthralled by the mystic teachings that these dossiers possess. The department of psychiatry should have a branch of specialization on *Pathanjali* teachings, as these dossiers are capable to manage various disorders of the mind. The dualistic outlook of man, as mind and body, with its antecedent neurotic disorders can be managed well by *Astanga Yoga.* Neuro-Psycho Spiritualism, a mix of the east and west, could well manage the monastic view of *Athman,* to both, the body and the mind. Some true psychiatric disorders do require continuous psychotropic drugs. One among the many causes for later-expressed disorders is due to the altered chemical contents inside the brain. Hence, the present mental health professionals boasting about their capability to provide total happiness to the depressed is in doubt. Modernisation has resulted in men possessing unexplained fears. There is a reason for this. Urban modernisation has led to a vertical growth rather than longitudinal growth. Vertical growth leads to loss of reality as man finds himself being socially subtracted, because a vertical urbanite dweller who has higher lodgings loses sight of the roots of his life below. The greater the heights the man achieves, he lives on simulated surroundings, rather than reality. A man living in the higher echelons of society clips his own social wings to avoid flight, to restrain oneself. Flying from heights could injure the man, as he has too much in stake. I do not mean that the proficient man should restrain from growth or confine to his limitations. Neither do I mean that we all should go and live in huge caves and start life afresh, as in the Stone Age period. What I actually mean is that we have to acutely ponder on the human's vertical growth. Today, architects construct buildings with hundred storeys to keep their cliental as comfortable as possible, but they are unable to provide happiness, which the people have to possess. This is exactly what I mean when I say that the human's horizontal growth is required for our peasant minds. To put in perspective, the complicated urban lifestyle of today has changed according to the people's attitude. After achieving every given comfort, people yet have some sorrow; this is where the mental health professionals have a role to play.

Hence, any attempt by these professionals to provide maximum comforts certainly leave with few discomforts to which is Yoga, a cliché in our modern language. My elucidations on Yoga have been covered extensively in my first book, *Parivarthana* (the change).

However, the answer to today's problems is not that simple, the answers provided until now lack scientific proofs. The answer I am seeking is more of an integrative approach or a mixed approach to the present-day elusive happiness. Aptly, could we call this path as neuro-psycho-spiritualistic science? This is a new field in which a scientist, scholar, philosopher, sociologist and spiritualist work together in an integrated manner to help overcome the sorrows of life. This science cannot be a proof-oriented field, but the study of this field is more of a parody. It is like inconclusive evidence of sound proof. Hence, the explanations what I could provide here are near to the truth or merely the absolute. The available non-scientific proof-oriented knowledge studies, regarding our worries and happiness, are vast. It is humanly impossible to cover the entire scriptures available and to apply the same to our entire life, to bring happiness. Hence, there should be a medium to have happiness. This medium is not just the vague study of mythological, religious, cultural and scientific books. I am cautious to introduce too much logic because the understanding of all these knowledge-oriented books provides us only meanings and not the required happiness. After all 'logic' is nothing but definition to a thing. Hence, I suggest that science in its simplest form is a myth and a cause for many of the ignorance we harbour. I have tried to explain the same in my first book *Parivarthana* (the change), for understanding *Athman* and also to understand reincarnation scientifically.

AGO BRAHMAN (Infinite Cosmos)

Nowadays, finding absolute happiness is like searching the root of *Ago Brahman*. It has been said in our *Naadu Nudi* (local language) that one should not try to find the roots of woman, wine and water. Hence, probably none of us is ready to find the roots of these three "W'S." If someone is always smiling and calling himself as blissful, it is appropriate to call him as schizophrenic. Hence, to be called normal, what he would require is minimum amount of happiness. In these changing trends, people have sufficient money to purchase everything, except happiness. I acquired this happiness through a lot of reading. I am comfortable to write on the complexity of life. I find happiness to discover the meaning of the many words and phrases present in the Veda and Puranas. I began to relate to these discovered meanings in this vast life. This reading habit of mine has helped me to understand the present complicated life in its simplest terms. Honestly, I found a change in myself after making a choice to use these learnt meanings for a positive approach in this negative interactive world. Application of these discovered meanings to my gawky life soothed my brain. This virtue I developed has brought me solace but not true bliss, which I really do not want. Therefore, this knowledge of mine motivated me to find meaning to such patterns, words or names, which are present in the past scriptures, for example, Yama (Lord of *Naraka* – hell). I have tried to provide meaning to the role of this King.

His name is often a part of our daily conversation. What would Yama mean to us? Invariably, the orthodox people in my country are scared of this king, but the role of this king, Yama, is an amazing concept, on which we must meditate to understand our ever-complicated lifestyles (Yama is one of the topics in my second Kannada book, *Manassu Mrudanga*).

THE KUTEERA (Sacred School)

In the east or in the west, from time immemorial, the saga of knowledge, their meanings and their insights have been passed from one generation to the next by sacred schools. Though the knowledge are in encrypted form, they generally try to convey meaning to life, try to explain nature at its best, with the help of various thoughts, address the differences in the world, try to solve complicated matters and also give maximum impetus to unearth the knowledge of the infinite universe. Earlier, this was possible bypassing of information from *Guru* (master) to *Chela* (student). It was known as "*Guru–Chela* relationship." Later, the student was called *Snatha* (sacred student), a person who had followed the utmost *Brahmacharya* (celibacy) path and was true to his *Guru.* Teachings in those days were provided in completely residential settings, outside or inside the *Kuteera* (thatched small house). The same concept has been adopted by our present-day educational system, where they call such centers as post-graduation centers or *Snatha Kothara.*

Nowadays, there are only a few *Kuteera* schools that still exist in a few remote places. It is difficult to obtain their details. Sages and Gurus of such centers had the extraordinary knowledge of perception and reasoning. They never taught their disciples physics, biology or chemistry. The secretly maintained the written scriptures of many sages that were transferred from one generation to the next in a ZIP format or in a coded form, as in our software. All these complicated coded folders were analysed and decoded. Each person, who had access to these folders, explained them in their own individualistic texts and such writings are called as *Bhashyas* (interpretations). Therefore, we have different kinds of *Bhashyas* in different religions and in different formats of the same religion. With due respect to all religions and languages, all religions try to convey the same concepts about the source of life, its progress and finally decay. Any philosophical approach along these lines would invite criticisms and arguments. These critics have refined our thinking and have made us to live successfully, though not peacefully. Therefore, understanding is an ever going and moving construct and finally it helps us reach a state of happiness though not absolute *Ananda* (total happiness).

PRALAYA (A Distant Possibility)

Life is divided into different branches. Life is divided into the past, present and future. Time is set on the ever moving or changing properties of the universe, also the physical and psychological changes within us. The same time is obsolete in deep space where there are no visible particles. The infinite space is divided only into two parts, they are *Vyaktha* (seen) and *Avyaktha* (not seen). The space is not a vacuum but it is full of electromagnetic energy with charged quanta, which holds the whole Universe as a single unit. I read an article regarding vacuum, it said that if by any chance or means the energised existing particles in space doubles its weight, then, it can create an enormous vacuum into which our life and matter could be sucked. This is what *Pralaya* (Dooms day) means and this is how *Pralaya* could be a possibility. At this juncture, I ask the readers to think more pragmatically about *Pralaya*.

OPEN MEDITATION (My Invention)

Life in the environment can be explained by the relation between living and non-living objects, and their intangible associations with the society. This type of bondage that evolved was called relationships. This could be between people related by blood and those not related by blood, and also between living and non-living objects. As per science, life is explained on three counts, that is, by its origin, its continuous developmental process and finally its decay.

In anthropology, life was studied by the different genera and species. The new or Neo Encephalon in our brain is a very recent entity when compared to the brain of other living species. Brain existed before the mind evolved. For example, observable brain or nerve components are seen in amoeba, as well as in many insects. Here the mind exists only for survival and procreation. The evolved mind is different when compared to insects and animals because the evolved mind has to execute certain positive functions with the real purpose of mind existence being questioned. So, man never questions his own mind and hence he finds no happiness. No health professional could provide the previously mentioned total happiness at any point of time. This happiness cannot be bought. This possible happiness has to be searched (Seeker) individually. He should understand what he has searched (Seek). He should observe, realise and adopt (Seeked) what he meant on his search. This is what I teach my clients and this is what I mean as Yoga. This process of search, I call as Open Meditation. I am pleased for my invention called Open Meditation, which I narrate extensively in my official third book *Prarthana* (the prayers). I am happy if my concept on Open Meditation multiplies, gets divided and is dispersed to the people in this world.

Mind, which is a part and parcel of our body, is discussed under the chapter of psychological evolutional development from low instincts to reformations and finally to high transformations. In spite of our knowledge, we are stuck at the instinctive level, which is not appreciated by the present-day society. Changing trends in life resulted in adjustments in the ever-changing environment with accompanying stress. As we are all stuck in this primitive level, the techniques we adapt to find relief from our stresses have become weird or abnormal. Methods to cope, which we learn under stress, are not explained by any Natural Law. The relievers for stress are neither explained by the Statutory Law. Inadequate coping and relieving methods for the innumerable stresses that we face in this ever-complicated life lead to more confusion, high anxiety or severe depression. To overcome this confusion, anxiety and depression, we require a catalytic interface for our healthy survival. This catalyst, in the present circumstances, I could imagine of only the 'bond', life bondage or a positive bondage. The evolutionists have many theories regarding the evolution of dense body to a free mind. Anthropologists have explained this in length. They wrote this after observing our real struggle, the competition we face and Nature's demand expected of us. Ultimately, we are all sure that this wonderful Universe is made up of opposites, connected by its gross functions, by its subtle threads and by many strong elementary relations, which are Omnipotent, Omniscient and Omnipresent.

THRISHUL
(The Shiva's Divine Weapon)

The conceptual thought of life and matter originated from the old trilogy, as per *Shiva Purana* (story on Shiva), which symbolically represents the *Thrishul* and also the three *Vibhuthi Namas* on *Linga*, which is yet to be unraveled by the present-day scientists in our newly built high profile laboratories. At *CERN*, they simply failed in recreate Higgs Boson particle or God's particle. The concept of *Nama* (horizontal mark) on *Linga* or on Shiva's portrait provides a mystical view to this world. The top mark or the top *Nama* (mark) is for the heavenly world, the center *Nama* represents the earth and the lower *Nama* means the dark side of the evil world. This concept is today represented by the left and right wings of our political scenario. There is also an interesting story for the presence of left and right wings in today's politics.

For millions of years in our evolutionary process, there was a time when the use of soap and paper was a distant dream for our ancestors. Somehow, they had known that their hand could transmit diseases because of cleaning the anal orifice after defecation. These medieval people avoided the usage of hand that was used to clean buttocks for all other social activities. Those who had used the right or left hand to clean for thousands of years had this encrypted in the brain, which was later mapped onto the successive genes resulting in being left handed or right handed today. It was a natural selection. If a reader is interested in my statement, he should definitely search for Anthropological books. Today, we call people with bad taste and negative feelings as leftists and people with positive feelings and good taste as rightists. On this assumption, left is adverse and right is right. Probably, I assume that Shiva's *Thrishul* would convey the same explanation. The center, pointing structure is for harmony; left is for that which is not correct and right is for the correct. It is interesting to note that the eye of Shiva is presumed to be situated in the middle of *Nama.* This explains the vision of doer *(Drishta)* enjoying the *Drishti* (sight) on all these three planes.

If we delve a little deeper into this concept, the top and the bottom marks *(Namas)* have no such eyes, because for a person to view infinite dark matter above and limited darkness below is impossible. This dark matter, which we are not able to see, is most powerful and highly ill understood. This is exactly the reason why, as per our Hindu traditional teaching, we owe our respect to two Gods. Traditionally, in Hindu culture, people worship these two Gods. The first God is the God *Kala Bhairava*, who depicts the space or the dark matter above, and another God is the God *Patheleshwara,* who represents the unseen world below. Both these two places are untouched by mankind. That is why they are elevated to the status of God but not those on the earth, because the wicked man has contaminated the earth with their evil mind. This does not mean that man has not achieved anything. Proportionately, the bad has overtaken the good on this God-gifted Earth. Meanwhile, man too has been contaminated, and hence, as per Vedic teachings, man is not equal to God. It is only by being pure, like pure ghee, by the mind can a man be called as a person of God. This is possible only when a man empties his mind from all worldly thoughts to attain a state of *Nirguna* (above all the three *Gunas,* that are, one—*Rajasic,* second—*Tamasic* and third—*Saathvic*). In this world, one of them who had achieved such a state was the great Buddha, whom we worship as the *Avathar Purush* (enlightened man) or the reincarnation of Lord Vishnu (one facet of many facets of God).

VEDHA
(Not Vadhe or to Kill)

When I delve into the past in the mythological world, the Gothic Dark Age had mysterious clouds in the sky that objectively caused ill or spilled evil all over. There was infatuated, instinctual, incest relationship with possible demonic progenies, and such a scenario required urgently a light of hope by an illuminating hero, who would arise out of such darkness and could wipe out the future dirty lives and possibly would create a current wonderful world with hopeful rays of good light all over. This is also true in many religious mythological stories of different religions and cultures. Hence, darkness is considered as bad and dangerous, and houses all evil forces. In truth, darkness is a beautiful subject to be researched as it contains enormous unseen and unfelt energy, which is useful for the future generations as a good source of energy. There is a reason as to why dark matter is gold in the future, as the available energy sources today are fast depleting.

Presently, the same trilogy that was discussed in the mythological medieval years holds good for three aspects. These are the infinite knowledge the *Brhaman* possess, as the top mark *(Nama)* implies. The corruptness or the darkness in which we are living is represented by the lower mark *(Nama)* and the eye in the middle mark *(Nama)* elucidates that in people, eyes are present only physically and by enlarge they are absent in the mind. In other words, our acuity of visionary perception is perfect, with an acute or narrow thinking.

The earth is a bright and shining object, where everything appears brilliant, but in actuality, we are blind to observe worldly things as bright. Hence, we have lost our analysing capacity to perceive. Our perception is distorted by the on-coming colourful illusions, and we find it difficult to nibble on the resourceful psycho-social sources to overcome the said illusions.

- ✓ The psycho-social sources are:
- ✓ To ensure a transparent thought.
- ✓ To be whole-hearted.
- ✓ To have a future visionary wish.
- ✓ To execute many good deeds.

This is where our ruling government governs badly and in turn executes horrible misdeeds on humans and allows the ignorant and the innocent to suffer. The Sun or the source of knowledge has driven mankind out of darkness but has failed to destroy the darkness inside the individual mind. There is a way to diminish our ignorance rather than completely wipe it out, and that instrument is only one, "Knowledge" acquisition. This acquisition is a possibility if we can achieve the same through our

- ✓ Broad observations.
- ✓ Mere acceptance with due consideration.
- ✓ Good reasoning of our thoughts.
- ✓ Considerate understanding after knowing.

Implementation of these within the structured society is the true instrument of wisdom to destroy the darkness present inside our mind-

- ✓ To discard possessed ignorance.
- ✓ Oblivion to human sufferings.
- ✓ To impart goodness to mankind.

These are the other instruments for us to adopt for attaining wisdom. Hence, I take this as an opportunity to explain Veda in my own terms. According to me, Veda is not *Vadhe.* The latter word signifies to destroy. The first word is to build the mystical future world.

Gurena Vedaha Gnanam Jayaath Gnaayethe.

Through Guru, the ancient Veda conveys that the knowledge is the basic concept of removing our own veil of our self-discovery path, not just to be a human but to become a superhuman.

SAMUDRA MANTHANA (The Churning of the 'Mind Ocean')

There is a good old analogy as to what came first? The matter or the life, whatever said and done, Chomsky's language interpretations are phenomenal in terms of the linguistic origin. He proposed that if language came from nowhere then how could a child understand semantics of an adult (when Lord Krishna was in foetus form, he was able to listen to the story told by his mother). Chomsky poses a question that after child grew as an adult, how he could commit gross mistakes in his language though he as a child would have not committed such mistakes. Hence, he says that the language is inherent and could be encrypted in the genes. He explains further that the language already there in coded form could be refined through interaction with the diverse environment for a better gene encryption in the future. This tendency would allow future progenies to become prodigies. Therefore, according to him, life came first and then matter.

According to Vedanthic explanations, the origin of our Sanskrit Grammar is from silence. The ancient scriptures have recorded that the Great Lord Hanuman, a Sanskrit scholar, could structure the grammar of the present-day Sanskrit scripture by just hearing the rumbling sounds of silence (*Shravana)*.Analysing the *Shravana* in the mind is called *Manana.* Reasoning on analysis is *Manthana.*

If this theory is true, then actually this theory is opposite to that of Chomsky's theory. The theories pertaining to life and grammar originated as a result of *Samudra Manthana* (churning of milky ocean) or the source of life, and if language evolving after the continuous strong friction of *Pancha Bhuthas* is true then Chomsky is right. Hence, thoughts regarding life on the earth are actually related to aliens on the part of erstwhile scientists. To think on varied lines Chomsky's thoughts allow the scientists, who probably believed that life existed from the time when the very speck of earth was thrown out from the mega explosion millions of years ago. There is another possibility of life origin, it is that life could have been in a dormant state inside the meteors and asteroids as cosmic eggs, and it could have ultimately collided with the earth and thus life was dispersed all over Earth like pollen grains as dispersed by a flower. After this ancient event took place, the earth got cooled, condensed and reached a state with suitable environment that enabled man to live and progress. This resulted in our life, growth and production of progenies. This is the reason for our fear of alien strikes because if an alien speck can produce humans like us then how much super intelligence with enormous power could the real aliens have possessed. The scientists are working day in and out to find if there is a possible alien existence in our outer inter-stellar space. In fact, how we existed is not known and neither do we know the real source to our varied languages, but we can leave these arguments to the scientists and the professors. For a man to exist and live happily, there should be a catalytic medium. This catalyst could be 'nature's perfect harmony.' Language is a basic necessity for communication; hence, to bring harmony in the society, language should not be a barrier.

MOUNA (The Silence)

Lord Buddha was one who had not bothered about

- ✓ The beauty of his language.
- ✓ The treasury of the words he had.
- ✓ The love for the poems he wrote.
- ✓ The value of his sentences.
- ✓ The opinion of his expressions.

His preaching to mankind was to follow a peaceful life with the least sorrow. Sorrow is the pre-supposed character of a living person and it is not good on our part to ask a person to throw away his sorrow in a wastebasket. Hypothetically, if this is done, then there could be a real headache or a real issue for the corporation to dispose this particular garbage bin. When mayors of metros, corporations and municipalities are not able to dispose garbage properly, can we imagine the plight of our sorrow added to this. Hence, live with sorrow and understand the sorrow by Buddha's *Suthra.* This understanding allows the person to be still, and in this stillness, one might find a little illumination to see reason to his object clearly. As a result of this, the future to the sorrow that was dark hitherto now looks bright. This is how one searches answers to his own sorrow while being in total stillness (*Mouna*).

During Buddha's period, several Greeko–Roman stalwarts established firmly their philosophy on life.

However, Buddha's teachings were the opposite of Greeko–Roman philosophy. Greeko–Romans had spread their philosophy on life's origin, the mind, the matter and metaphysics. The reader reading such wonderful works by Greeko–Romans got fascinated by their invention of meanings to the words they had and also for the innumerable logos they had left behind. The process of discussion on these logos was called as logic, which was subjected to arguments and condemnations. The philosophical work by the Greeko–Romans was looked upon as evil by their kings, both right and left wings. This was the time when paranoia and persecution were rampant. Hence, there was no peace. If we are able to go through the Upanishaths and the Puranas, we find discussion on life and matter but fail to find the logic behind them because their writings are written based only on God with no mention of science. This is exactly why our great *Rushis* were not persecuted. With this profound statement, I would like to mention that when science got well-founded and had a good foothold on the land of Law, the subtle peace in the society kept disappearing. That is why the present-day scientists fail to acquire or possess the needed peace. The mystique East teachings are neither based on evolution nor on science. The teachings are based on the *Thathath* (as we are). This was how *Thanthra* came into existence. Therefore, Buddha preached life first. He had said, "Be in life, you find the truth." Here truth is God and Science. I would like to clarify this statement for the clueless by providing a cocktail. This cocktail is a smoothening mix of the teachings of the east and the west, to understand our life best.

YOGA (In its true Perspective)

On thinking about philosophy, I thought that philosophy was meant only for the intelligent people. As I was not intelligent in my college days, philosophy was difficult to understand. Many earlier friends had termed philosophy as a puzzle; now I feel that what they said was true; it is truly a puzzle and hence I thought it worth to rack my brains to understand the philosophy. I want to be a seminarian though I am not. For this, I was reading about Brenton's work; he is a psychiatrist from Vienna who had magnetised and mesmerised some of his greatest contemporary personalities like Sigmund Freud and other psychiatrists, including some philosophers. He was the one who had worked on, studied and wrote about logic behind a language. He was deeply involved in exploring the reasoning techniques (a posteriori) in relation to sensuality of a human. He had found that human intentionality like "Thinking" had always prior mental images. These images have oriented towards pleasure seeking, to satisfy human instincts. If these two cognitive constructs are not congruent then either of them would be termed as meaningless. For all our intentional behaviours, there must always be a purpose. On discovering this meaning, if there is sycophancy, then a person's behaviour could eventually become an antisocial behaviour. Therefore, a combination of maladjusted social behaviours could lead to many personality malformations with criminal implications. Such examples are the gruesome sexual assaults or psycho thrills that are committed. The language disorder in schizophrenia, such as formal thought disorder, might also be due to this non-congruency. It is fine for a philosopher or for a psychiatrist, but what does actually work at a neuro-anatomical structure with chemico-physiological changes? Neuro-anatomists, neuro-physicists and neuro-chemists should work towards discovering such a tract of incongruities in schizophrenics.

To my knowledge, till now, our scientists have not isolated intricate neuronal tracts, which are the basis for our incongruence in our nervous system. When they find these anomalous tracts with many deviant personalities, medically they could be subjected to some kind of pinpoint psycho-surgery to relieve them from such abnormalities, which are different from our old radical psychosurgeries. The present-day psychosurgeries by neuro-surgeons could result in more cerebral damage. The previously mentioned fine neuro-surgeries could bring down the post-surgical apathy and observable inertia. This explains that linear radiation from an X-ray accelerator is different from the conventional cobalt radiation for management of cancerous growths, by which we can minimise the destruction of healthy tissues and prevent post-radiation side effects. Until that is done, we have to rely on psycho-pharmacological drugs, which have adverse effects on the body. If such discoveries take place, neuro-surgical procedures would be the right choice; until then, Yoga can be implemented hypothetically to suppress or not to activate such tracts by some kind of mind stimulation techniques. If our new psycho-pharmacological drugs and new frontiers of neuro-surgical approach fail, then it could lead to the beginning of a new era of non-pharmacological or non-surgical approach to treat and manage various mental illnesses by different kinds of Yoga. My Open Meditation could be one method of the many frontiers of Yoga.

PATHANJALI MAHARUSHI (The Grand Father of Psychiatry)

While reading *Pathanjali Suthras* under the topic *Kaivalya Pada,* I found a parlance to the previously mentioned neuro-physiological idea in one of the dossiers, of which I am going to mention.

Nirmana Chitthanyaa Asmitha Maatrat.

This *Suthra* means that a created mental image always or surely has a prerogative sensuous phenomenon. The *Suthra* continues to say:

Pravruthi Bhede Prayojakam Chitham Ekam Anekam.

This *Suthra* means, thus the created thought of an intention is a result of the previous image of sensual origin and has many expressions to the sensuality already created.

There are many other *Suthras* of *Pathanjali* that explain the *Yogic* path by which an egoistic man could come out of his bondages by understanding his own self-egoistic weird thoughts. This is possible by performing intense meditation so as to bring a change in himself from bad to good. This exercise would allow him to view life better or to realise the cause and effect of the world. *Pathanjali* teaches that the impressions and memories are present in the same consciousness. Man also should realise that the past and future exist in his own mind. Man also should know that the properties or the *Dharma* of this dynamic world always keep expressing in various things in his artificial mind but not in his absolute mind. Hence, to live with this reality for our survival it is an ongoing process of

- ✓ Earnest effort.
- ✓ Maximum struggle.
- ✓ Relentless work.
- ✓ Hard persuasion.
- ✓ Strong determination.
- ✓ Continuous practice.

All these attributes take *Drishta* into the path of true reality to achieve *Jeevana Mukthi* or life liberation. People should not immerse in river Ganga (river Ganges) to get *Moksha* (liberation). *Na-layak* (useless people) people do practice this. My advice is not to escape from the hard realities for attaining knowledge. We all know this is a difficult process. Invariably, we find simple ways to change. Brutes and thugs make their living by mugging, subverting and cheating innocent people. This cheating or conning is a problem that they have but I would like to come back to this wonderful world in my next *Janma* (generation) for something to leave on Earth, because as of now I am not going to leave anything.

YAMA DHARMARAJA (The Lord of Hell)

I do not know who wrote Upanishath. Before I delve on the *Upanishath*, I want the reader to understand that Mythology is different from Upanishath. The Mythology is more iconographic and it is written in the scriptures on the experiences of Mythological powers. Hence, I presume, Gods did exist earlier than the *Rushis* who wrote the Upanishath literature. The authors (*Rushis*) who wrote these scriptures and their past video clips are not available today to confirm or to prove their existence. The content of these scriptures really baffles a naive reader. When I superficially glanced on these writings, I marveled, and was amazed and astonished for the hidden meanings that these dossiers possess. I am not a pundit to go into the depth of the Upanishaths. The *Bruhad Aranyaka Upanishath* was written by many sages with extraordinary vision in the *Arranya* or the forest after they had fulfilled all their earlier obligations; they unraveled and tried to convey meaning to life, world, planets, death, birth, sex, vital force, etc. through their writings. As I read through the Upanishath, I found an illuminating similarity regarding the language in one of the *Suthra* in *Bruhad Aranyaka Upanishath*. According to this, the intensions of humans expressed through speech are about wants and dislikes, and they are always from prior thoughts. If what I say is true, then the spoken language is secondary to breath or *Udgaetha* and that is why in the *Upanishath* a lot of importance had been given to the *Prana* or the breath. In terms of evolutionary process, this *Udgaetha* is relatively new and can be related to Freudian super ego. The old, which has demonic virtues, are the senses or *Pancha Indriyas*. These are our instincts. Ego is a catalytic agent, which is nascent at present and which works between these two, identity and superego. This subtle or spiritual dimension of language can be dangerous when used ineffectively. This dimension should be excised very judiciously and cautiously, because the speech or the *Udgaetha* is always expressed as breath latticed with inner sensuous aroma, and hence words reflect the sanctum sanctorum of a person. His deeds reflect the shining inside. Independence of either (identity, ego) is dangerous to man, detrimental to the society and to life in general. Hence, the *Prana Yama* has an astounding role to play in our life.

The Yama means morality over the *Prana*. This has an important meditative value in our daily interactive life. For an inquisitive reader probably a question on 'Yama' could arises: Who is this Yama? And what does he means to us? No man on earth would match Yama because he is God of Death. Who wishes his own death? Every one of us wants to live long. For me, Yama always was an amazing character. Frankly, I do not know about the first man on this earth. I am not an authority to answer many questions like: When did he live? When did he die? Unlike god who has no death, the first person on this earth definitely would have died. After being born on earth, a person has to get contaminated as per the Vedanthic teachings. To mark the occasion of man's contamination, we celebrate *Purudu* or inauspicious period. This is done on two occasions: when a child is born and also when a man dies. These periods are inauspicious because the new-born child is getting contaminated with the illusion or the *Maya.* The same process is described after the death of a person as he has already contaminated this world, and when he leaves this world, he is going to contaminate the world above, which is always clean. Hence, the first person on this earth who had lived is not pure but contaminated. There is a reason as to why this person was not pure. To promote the life for his future generations, this person would have indulged in sex; if he had not loved, we would not be on earth. This is probably the only mistake he could have committed. When he was not completely pure, then, after his death, he could only find the way to *Naraka* or hell. Being the first man, he should have been the Boss or the King of *Naraka.* It is assumed that after the first man died, all further births are getting more contaminated by their mind. Hence, many of us today possess corrupt and crooked minds. As the King in his kingdom, he has to build a palace with *Manthri* (home minister) and soldiers to receive and control the anarchists who enter hell after their deaths. Today in our country, anarchism is directly proportional to intelligence. To control such people in a Kingdom above, there should be a rule of law. To execute such a law, this King has to perform *Dharma* (uplifting the parliamentary credentials). The *Dharma* is all about the Yama or the morality. Hence, the first King was named as Yama Dharmaraja. Therefore, by understanding this analogy, this King is supposed to be near to God. This King was having good principles and virtues of high moral standards. This is how Yama or the near moral person was the King empowered to rule anarchists like us after our death. For me, the *Naraka Kandha* (evil world) is a myth.

As long as I am wise, then this present world is *Sundara Kandha* (beautiful world) to me. The King Yama is a *Mithra* (friend) for the wise and *Shathru* (enemy) for an anarchist. Hence, I suppose or presume that the control over the *Prana* or the morality of speech, the Prana Yama, would be a main impetus to the society.

Yo He Vai Jestam Cha Srestamcha Vedaha, Jestascha Strestascha Swa Am Bhavathi, Pranoha Vai Jestascha, Srestascha, Jestascha Strestatha Cha Swa Am Bhavathi; Api Cha Yesam Bubbhuhu Ati, Ya Evam Vedaha.

He (the creator) knows the oldest of oldest and also that of high standard and that is the breath. Breath is the greatest in all beings on earth. Thus, the *Prana* or the life source is supreme. Hence, speech is the greatest of all, according to Veda.

The *Suthra* explains that if speech is not linked with will or inner senses, then the expressed speech does not mean anything. Hence, the person's *Prana* (action and speech) would be at fault. This is being discussed by science today, which explains the importance of sensual neuronal integration for the production of correct speech with expression. Meditating on *Prana* would bring cheer to life. Today our problem is that we do not discuss the real issues and we have a naive way by which speech is rectified; the differences we possess on a day-to-day basis should change instantaneously into no differences. Actually, *Prana* Yama is not just about inhaling air and speaking all ill. People speak but never convert their speeches to deeds and thus a difference exists that is dangerous to the society. I believe that if both go hand in hand, the prosperity in terms of mental and physical health, individually and collectively, would improve.

THE CONFESSIONS – NOT TO REMEMBER (To Meditate On)

Invariably, men look miserable in spite of their strong memories and their extraordinary remembrances. I love 'forgetfulness' for the same reason. A friend of mine boasts of his excellent memory; but, this results in him remembering only the quarrels with his wife. This quarrel would keep inflating like a balloon; but it would be deflated the instant she refused to take part with him in his bedroom. His wife consults a psychiatrist for a method or a drug by which her husband's memories can be erased permanently. However, the forgetful psychiatrist had already forgotten the name of the drug to be prescribed to her husband's problem. She went on meeting many psychiatrists to find a permanent solution to her husband's memory. At last, she could find one psychiatrist who could help her. She was happy with the medicines he had prescribed because this psychiatrist was intelligent enough to remember the names of the drugs that he had prescribed to her husband. The drugs that were prescribed were to relieve her husband's obsession. I think that the reason behind this antidepressant prescription was because this psychiatrist thought that her husband was suffering from memory ruminations. Candidly, her husband's depression was a result of her nagging attitude. Her husband tried the SSRI'S prescribed by the psychiatrist. To her surprise, his memory doubled. Now, she visited another psychiatrist. The drug prescribed by this psychiatrist was again SSRI'S that were used for obsessions, which did improve her memories and made them more vivid. Actually, by consuming this antidepressant drugs she brought back

- ✓ Her hidden memories of her husband insulting her.
- ✓ Her memories of comparisons made by her husband with other women.
- ✓ Her memories of the six-pack body he possessed.
- ✓ Her memories of her husband's under-performance in his business.
- ✓ Her memory of her husband's declining manhood.
- ✓ Her memories of failed intimate love by the husband.
- ✓ Her memories of her passionless husband, etc.

All these memories she would have forgotten if she had been mistakenly drugged by the antipsychotics prescribed by her treating psychiatrist. The antipsychotics are a blessing in disguise for the rural patriarchs, as this would have brought respite. The patriarch's spouses would be silent after they were prescribed antipsychotics. This management could have resulted in the rural women becoming inactive and their husbands would have an excuse to marry another woman. Please excuse me for making this statement because as a practicing psychiatrist, I know I am not above God, and I too have made many mistakes. These mistakes have helped me to manage patients better as days progressed. This husband–wife analogy shows that the memories are deeply embedded in the dark space of our minds, which would keep surfacing on a day-to-day basis resulting in continuous fights. Therefore, to pacify, a small antidepressant course or useful discussions on the issues between them would perhaps bring little solace to both. This solace without drugs would have brought healthy conjoint life attributes later. Hence, my advice to couples would be to remember the past events and keep quarrelling rather than indulging in fierce fights. After all, their quarrels could bring them more intimate. There is a saying, where hate prevails, love does exist (love and hate relationship).

Lord Buddha is one of the great sages who had erased all his memories through his intense meditation. His mind was like 'a vacuum' or *Shuunya* state. By this technique of meditation, his mind would have sucked the compassionate dynamics of the world easily. If by chance his mind was filled with only memories and obsessions, he would have remained as the King permanently. This is the reason why he is called as reincarnation of Lord Vishnu or *Brhaman* the pure. Hence, he was emitting only compassion and forgiveness, but not reflections. It is true that Lord Buddha had forgotten to be himself, so he could mix with *Prakruthi* (nature) at ease. He was the real *Yogi,* an enlightened master, who wanted to master the art of *Thy*. He succeeded in his enlightenment by practicing *Jeevana Mukthi.* Lord Buddha was an icon not to be forgotten but currently we find Buddhas of little stuff.

Another friend of mine was reproached daily by his wife; he was treated badly and was driven out of his house to bring back his love for her. This friend had totally forgotten his wife's love. He had no time for love because he was in love with his computers and the internet. There is an art to help forget. This art is called "confessions." Confessions are made by the husbands to their wives in darkness in the confines of their bedrooms, because wives are so intelligent that if their husbands confess in light, they can make out immediately the split nature or two faces of their husbands. Husbands do confess but their body languages never coincide with their words, hence it is a pseudo-confession. Confessions bear the truth when confessed from the heart. General confessions made by convicts to the judges are invariably by force. Our police inefficiency and legal inattentiveness allow a real culprit to escape. In this way, a slight punishment buries an innocent person's innocence because of the inefficient policy institutions in our country. It is the efficiency and the knowledge of the police that unravels the truth in any given country. The inefficiency on our part or our system allows a villain to be masked, as we see in our *24/7 TV* channels. We have temples, churches and mosques not for praying but to confess. This is how our people develop their mind sets notoriously to increase their ill practices. People practice so because God who is present in all these places is invisible and also one should know that God is devoid of eyes. Wives do visit prayer halls to seek solace, while husband's visit places of worship only to confess. Hence, we are all free to enter these temples to confess. Confessions are nothing but a method to purge ourselves, which Sigmund Freud called as "Free Association*.*" When we purge, we are relieved from our stress. This type of phenomenon of total bliss could be experienced by a constipated man after defecation.

Dear readers, many a times the confessions that we want to make are not true confessions but still they are confessions, just an iota of truth. When these confessions are not true, retaining the truth would choke us from within. At this juncture, people consult a psychiatrist. Until this time, the psychiatrist is generally latent in the public domain. Professionals have many instruments in their pocket to relieve all these stresses depending on the wealth of the client. The level of deliverance by psychiatric help depends on the rate of consultation. Today, any good speaker would be considered as a counsellor; actually, they are pseudo-counsellors to those who are stressed. Recently, there was an article written on counselling. The delivery of structured client-oriented counselling by the professionals would help psychologically the patients better. Unprofessional counselling approach would harm them more. Why have I made this point? For counselling a stressed person, it could be by a friend, a teacher, a doctor, a lawyer or a relative. Thus, he need not be necessarily a professional. If this counsellor is a *Swamy* (astrologer) who could relieve stress by forbidden means, which depended on their adrenalin and oxytocin levels (recent sex scandals reported in media), there could be problems for the man who wanted his stress to be relieved. This actually would help the stressed man or woman by way of stimulating large nerve fibers on the skin where there is release of endo-morphins or endorphins, which would lead to a sort of temporary euphoria with total relaxation. A man indulging in such acts of help to his clients should ask himself whether he is fit enough to suggest his clients for such acts. This is true for the professionals too. If such a kind of treatment continues by the professionals, one day they may be projected as heroes. This type of practice is a taboo all over the world. The ethos and morality oscillate between the consciousness of the indulger and the temporary circumstantial orgasmic high in an indulgee. The temporary psychological relief to their obsessions is mediated by nerve fibers on the skin, for example, *Rekhi, Kundalini* Stimulation, *Thanthric* Sex, etc.

GATE THEORY (The Art of MASSAGE)

Under the Vedanthic teachings, the art of stimulation of peripheral nerves or this mode of treatment or management had been considered as of lowest value. Whatever may be the explanation given by the scholars who practice these methods, for example many schools of body therapists who claimed to have relieved body pains of their clients, being a psychiatrist, I would consider the relief that their clients get is by the Gate Theory (theory pertaining to secretion of endorphins and self-analgesics through body nerve stimulation). This is a temporary phenomenon, which would later convert into obsessions and compulsions. To render permanent remedy to our stress (the multiple body pains is one of the symptoms of stress) would be more difficult. Presently, to penetrate the skill of meditation is difficult (due to the paucity of time and patience) by the patients or clients; hence, they would go and seek the previously mentioned management method for their immediate pain relief. The media's curiosity and their neighbour's influence would accentuate many innocent men's life to suffer from such cure mongers. In these relationships, clients are responsible to realise the nature of such treatments. Hence, confessions are rare, and when confessed, they are considered as rape (as per the recent amended law of the Supreme Court).

Confessions have no place in our judiciary system. The convictions are always on the basis of good investigations.

The testimony is on the basis of scientific evidences and proofs provided to the courts. We have numerous Sherlock Holmes and they possess state-of-the-art techniques related to forensic technology, but still we do not use our intelligence and investigative equipments due to the constrained obsessions and hidden compulsions. Efficient brains are worried and unscathed by their honest work. Hence, all who get caught are masked in front of the media until they are proved beyond doubt of their act. Such heroes should be masked because he could be an innocent man. There is another advantage of this mask for a man who is caught on a criminal prima facie evidence wherein this man, so-called a convict, could be a real convict who could sketch and escape beyond the judiciary (our corrupt bureaucrats' could have a role to play for convicts to escape).When the investigation agency investigating a particular case fails to provide proper proof in the court of law, then the law enforcers enforce the technique of 'confession.' Under these conditions, this 'confession' would be an appropriate word for an inquiry officer. This is how our jails have become big mental asylums. A bonded and harassed innocent man is a virtual mad man. This is exactly what I want to convey. When there are no suitable people and also forensic laboratories, this nation turns ultimately into a nursing home for the body and the mind ailments. Let us have a distant vision in our life to convert our big national nursing home into a psychological care home. It is interesting to note that each member of this mega home is a learned counsellor. Lastly, it is for the reader to confound what Confession is all about.

THU THU MAIN MAIN (The Malicious)

Epics like Mahabharata and Ramayana are true stories today. Bygone sages wrote these scripts as they knew that these epics would be an infinite one. The past sages would have had long Hublescopic vision. Quarrels exist for two surreptitious reasons. One is because of deep remembrance and another is because of our confessional attitude. It is a tragedy to blame *Aham* (ego) for our present misunderstandings. *Thu Thu, Mei Mei* is our politicians' linguafranca. I would like to relate the obsessive remembrance to bioscopic post-traumatic stress disorder (PTSD). The picture frame is a perfect *70 MM* with one shot and no retakes. Petty misunderstandings that occur are because of the following reasons:

- ✓ Husband forgetting to offer *Mallige* (jasmine) flowers.
- ✓ Husband not serving a cup of hot tea after a day of ordeal.
- ✓ Unkempt house because of excess usage of Facebook or Twitter.
- ✓ Not sharing salary when in need.
- ✓ Not allowing balancing based on their hierarchy.
- ✓ Discontent on material transactions.
- ✓ Pent up skewed emotions.
- ✓ Cross-checking beliefs.
- ✓ Distrusting the thoughts and actions, etc.

This story would never end, and completes on a bad note. The person who enjoys the most is the neighbour. If there were no arguments in another person's family, his neighbour would not be at peace. This *Pari Passu* of life is unfortunate and as a psychiatrist I do not find any immediate remedial measures for this present menace. It is free *Tamasha* for the neighbour whereas a terrible ordeal for the true actors (couple). Heaven on earth for such couples is a far reality.

Many successful heroes never think about their future negatively. For those who have not succeeded, there could be a ray of hope, a distant possibility where a drug would cause selective forgetfulness. The most powerful bad memory is that a good thought that could be just a dream. I have a story to mention. I was a hero after a youth had read my first Kannada book *"Manassu Mandaara."* He was visibly enthralled on reading my book, and he wanted me to inaugurate a youth organisation in his village. There was a reason for this. For the youth of the village, I was like a Demi God due to my Vedanthic narrations in the book. In this book, I had injected Vedantha into my professional experiences. This young student, studying in his final year *BA,* Mr X, is an ardent believer of his Community Guru and was fascinated by the contents of my book. I was utterly confused after this boy's suicide, whether his liking my book was secondary to his hypo-manic state or his pure knowledge base. I feel sorry for the poor soul that has left to God's abode. I wish he would have survived because he had a vision of constructing an empire called *Sneha* (friendship). The organisation that I was going to inaugurate was named "*Sneha Samrajya.*" The function was well attended by the village youth; speakers invited were relevant to the present-day problems of the youth and the function was conducted jubilantly and ended on a good cultural note. I was honoured and considered by them as *Gourava Adhyaksha* (honorary president). For me, my designation was a blessing in disguise. On this day, I felt I too had fans. Mr X and his friends' organisation's vision was:

- ✓ to spread harmony.
- ✓ to educate the rural mass regarding politics.
- ✓ to explain regarding grants awarded by some financial schemes of the Government, which could be used by the youth.
- ✓ to perform street plays depicting ignorance on mental illnesses, spreading *Saha Balve* (harmonious life) and *Saha Dharma* (equality and religious oneness), etc.

In the middle of the function there was a *Samvadha* (question and answer session) between the youth and the speakers. I was asked a long question about training to the youth. He had asked "How could oneness be achieved?" My simple answer was "Easy, one could achieve oneness by detachment and being non-hating." As usual my Vedanthic answer welcomed cheers and as well as boos from the crowd. I failed to know how much the crowd would have understood my statement. Let me explain oneness in my own fashion, "Oneness could be a possibility by an innovated self-instrument, which would erase our bad memories, or a method in which we are able to learn the art of adapting to a selected painful memory." Therefore, in a nutshell, it explains that we always have bad memories, which would cause us to brood.

Today people are busy in piling up their earned money. Such stacked wealth is spent by their wards to buy drugs. A psychiatric drug would be a better option than drugs of addiction. In reality or in such circumstances, the psychiatrist is not approached by the public due to the taboo attached to them; hence, the nearest approach would be the prominent soothsayers. Such stacked money could instead have been spent on faith healers. Can astrologers talk about the neuro-anatomy, the neuro-chemistry and the neuro-physiology? The present problem with a psychiatrist is that he is not trained at a neuro-psycho-spiritual level. Hence, immediate training is required to fight the soothsayers.

At present, we have antidepressants that can wipe out obsessions but not our brooding. Pharmaceutical clinical research institutes should discover a drug molecule that can wipe out our brooding rather than our obsession. Obsession is a disease, but not brooding. A psychiatrist could manage an obsession better when compared to managing the mega social ills. The management of these evils would be by more of a servo-mechanism or by inclusive management colluding with all mental health professionals. I was going through the newspaper where a minister for education was talking as "No *Kesari Karana* (saffronisation)" in school textbooks. Primarily, I have a question to him, "What would *Kesari* colour stand for in our country (related to education)?" It is unfortunate to study in our country, as we are not taught about Krishna, Rama and the bygone great sages. All these should be introduced in our curriculum in simple terminologies and we also should highlight their virtues and should spread their values to the people in a phase-wise manner. Ancient scriptures should not be an abstract text to the common Indian youth. Abstract nature of these texts is for a *Pundit* or for a research scholar.

DANCE OF THE DEMOCRACY V/S DANCE AT THE STADIUM (Comparison)

The mythological Nataraja's dance over the *Rakshasha* (evil) body to the tunes of cosmic music comprising infinite strings was also called as Cosmic Dance. This dance is been said to be full of love, passion and compassion. Because of Lord's grace or dance, we are all somehow surviving with unseen social connections. Our creator has not forgotten us because he has to live; if he forgets us, then for all practical purpose He is dead. Hence, the Lord showers love on us and in turn we shower trash (organic waste and plastic) on Him. What a pity? In our day-to-day life, we keep observing overtly or covertly

- ✓ The dance of father against mother.
- ✓ The dance of husband against his wife.
- ✓ The dance between birds in love.
- ✓ The dance of the strong over the suppressed.
- ✓ The dance of the boss over his subordinates.
- ✓ The dance of the employees against their employer, etc.

Wherever we go, we dance to the tunes of the drums in that society. If I am not a dynamic dancer in this dancing society, I am perished. This is what Buddha said: Move, Connect and Enjoy. Ultimately, a dancer wants to achieve or to meet near total bliss. Dance is all-pervading; it is in the soul and the mind. We make others to dance to our tunes or we dance to the tunes of others. We boast as being one of the strongest and largest democratic country in this world, but, we dance in this society with our wings clipped and limbs amputated by this so-called democracy. We are fit to compete in Paralympics than in the main Olympics. That is why we have many medals in the Paralympics category but not in the Olympics category. Politicians dance to the tunes of:

- ✓ Religion.
- ✓ Cast.
- ✓ Creed.
- ✓ Power.
- ✓ Money.

Lord Nataraja dances on the previously mentioned *Rakshasa* (demon) to kill evil, but in our democracy, the politician dances over the taxpayer's body, who is actually a peasant, transparent to the core, common in his outlook and ignorant in his deeds, only to get re-elected. Our daily owes to God have reached the imaginary ears of the permanent deaf, but our words are heard by the ever-inattentive minds of these politicians only to con and cheat us more. In this dance of democracy, the taxpayer is taxing his patience not to the tunes of Bharatanatyam but he is dancing to the tunes of a jerky, nauseating and disturbing dance of suicides, homicides and innumerable incurable mental diseases. When there is rain in my town, I feel happy to skip my tennis sessions because of wet clay court conditions. I love going for a stroll inside the stadium, which is near to my town makeshift weekly market. It was Tuesday, on a scorching summer in May. The stadium seemed to invite me to make my observations. For my body and soul, walking would be more refreshing. It was a dance of happiness in me because only occasionally I visit the stadium, as otherwise I am more inclined to take a walk on the streets. The stadium was almost empty except for the regular users. All of them were new faces doing different antics to execute their exercise techniques. It was a dance because I never have seen such a scene with people walking on the streets. People who walk are usually slow or fast walkers, alone or in a group. People while walking walk with their strait jackets, but in the stadium they are unbounded, they are free to wear any type of clothes, and so they are not restricted in exhibiting their skills. The town stadium is mediocre, just big enough to burn our calories after two or three rounds of walking around the oval-shaped playground. I listened to the boastful whispers of those in their forties and fifties who were boasting that they had burnt five hundred to six hundred calories, but to me they looked weird with their belly protruding out from their body, like Lord Ganesha (God known for his belly). They walk and talk *"Neenu Estu Aasthi Madide?"*, meaning how much money you have earned until now? It is fortunate to find that the same boasting is not present among the professional athletes who are practicing; it is an unfortunate sight that I noticed, as there was no seriousness in their training sessions. The paradox is that the seriousness helps to bring self-laurels during their training sessions but calmness helps them in competitions to secure more medals for the country. This dichotomy in our athletes has robbed them of many medals. There are many more factors for non-achievement and hence beyond my explanation. In all, the weather was so cool by the sizzling dance of the athletes around me. In the stadium there were groups of friends walking and talking; I probably guess that their talk was related to their children's scholastic performance and mutual automatic acknowledgement. As I went on walking around the stadium, I found a person talking ill about one of his friend in his absence, to which his other friend was adding more *Masala*. I found another person walking and speaking on his mobile to his subordinate to check his accounts in various banks. I thought he would be a serious businessman. In one group, there was a discussion related to their political knowledge on the problems of our country. In another place, a walker in his forties was trying to solve his friend's family problems via the mobile phone like a real counsellor. For me, all these scenes were like many facets of the dance in the stadium. After I listened to this person's counselling technique via mobile phone, I felt that his technique of counselling was far better than my technique and it had really made me an incompetent psychiatrist.

There were many couples taking leaps and strides while walking. One husband (I presume) was dancing in his Kathak style; meanwhile, his spouse was exercising drills like in her school days. Another man in his fifties was exhaling with nasal secretion blowing like mist from his nostrils, and I thought that it was his style of performing *Prana Yama* (breathing exercise). Young athletes, two girls and a boy, in their twenties, were hopping up and down over spectators' stone benches. They were running for some time and then walking briskly for some moment; one boy exercising in that group was showing off his sweating body unconsciously so as to lure a girl who had come for a walk. In another place, I found a group aged in their forties and fifties swinging their arms up and down and their heads turning left and right discussing the present politico-social scenario of our state, etc.; I really enjoyed these scenes with one mega dance scenario in my mind. After I seriously collected and threaded these many pictures, frankly, it was like an inspirational learning movie. This I could do only by my mere observations. Still I felt that this dance in the stadium was far better than the dance of democracy. It is a paradox to know that people voted when the onion was priced at fifty to eighty rupees a kilogram and sold to the people, but the existing government lost in the election because of not being voted by the same people. This is what I want to convey when I mention the dance of democracy. Hence, what I would like to advice is to dance with the accompanying musical instruments of:

- ✓ Good virtues.
- ✓ Mediocre calmness.
- ✓ Little understanding.

Very less knowledge would make our lives dance difficult. The spectators are the living beings, non-living beings and *Panchabuthas* (five principle elements of nature) of our Mother Nature, who in turn enjoy viewing this Eureka dance.

"Let us dance to the tunes of our merged personality and not for someone's fancy."

BETTING AND GAMBLING (In Relevance to SAMUDRA MANTHANA)

I may fail to furnish literal meaning to 'betting', but to my knowledge, this word suggests 'surety' like "I bet on that." As per Buddha's teachings, this surety has no place in meditative dictionary. He says sureness leads to dullness, which is a hallmark of *Dummana* (sad and fear) of a person. The modern betting should be seen in many perspectives. As a practicing psychiatrist, my opinion about this betting is that it is a useful obsession and it should be not referred as obsessions. Little obsessions are required to overhaul human needs to sustain our dynamic life. Living is also an obsession, which is socially accepted, and any obsessive deviancy from the social framework is a taboo, for example, eating human flesh, which is permitted only with pygmies. Our living obsessions are not felt as obsessions as they are always marked with moral duties and responsibilities amid social obligations. They are all socially prescribed and de facto printed in our genes from generation to generation. To simplify the said factor further, I ask the reader to follow my statement. For a married man to look at his wife is not an obsession because it is socially permitted but looking at a neighbour's wife daily is an obsession and this draws a contrast in moral normality to abnormality. Frankly, every one of us is obsessive of a variety of pleasures in this world. It is a paradox that a huge and beautiful Taj Mahal was built on one man's emotion at the cost of the emotions of thousands of workers whose hands were chopped off, were killed or buried alive for only one obsession of this King, that the same structure should not be duplicated. Hence, the king who was building Taj Mahal was also sure of harbouring notorious mega-structural obsessions regarding its duplication. This is exactly the difference between an obsessive King and the great humble Buddha. Buddha was one who never had pleasurable obsession in his mind but had immense obsession for solving *Dhukha* (sorrow) in the society. His obsession on these lines enabled him to teach us only meditation for our betterment.

If I go back into the world of mythology, there was a *Yuga* where only *Bhakthi* and meditations prevailed among people. It is said that in this *Yuga*, Mother Earth was not organised properly. In this period, people were possessed or harboured double obsession of fear. The people of the bygone time were of only two types, *Asuras* and *Suras*, who indulged in blood bath as today's Naxals. Lord Vishnu (an important incarnated deity of life's progress) was compassionate enough to bring an existing amendment then to end killings by reincarnating himself to *Koorma Avathar*. This huge *Koorma* (turtle), the god almighty naturally, was a mythological platform or float in the *Ksheera Samudra* (milky sea) for an imaginary churning mega pole, which was churned by a big serpent *Adishehsa* (great serpent) by *Suras* on one side holding its tail and on the other side by *Asuras* holding on to the head to yield many good and bad materials churned out from the *Ksheera Samudra's* bottom. After churning the milky ocean, the knowledgeable *Suras* (Gods) chose eternal good to live and the ferocious *Asuras* (demons) chose evil material to kill and perish fast, as those chosen materials gave instantaneous pleasure and also instant death. Therefore, obsessions in men developed for one's possession and not as de facto cognizant. Hence, men did not like monotonous attitude, fixed aptitude and same behaviour. In this background, betting is prevailing from ages and it is not at all a new trend. From obsession, betting has converted into today's compulsions like corruption and sex. Betting can be stopped only when sex and corruptions are stopped, which is humanly impossible, and hence, one should not view betting as bad, but it is good when people view betting with their *Viveka* (discriminative power).

Having said all, as per Diagnostic Statistical Manual-5 (DSM-5), classification of psychiatric phraseology, basic good obsessions, which are necessary in a man's life, are also seen as abnormal. It is unfortunate to know that obsessions without emotions (automatic obsessions) too are going to be abnormal in this classification. The basic obsessions, which are tagged to negative emotions, are bad for a man to experience. If this statement holds good, then who is normal? What about betting, gambling and other socially accepted compulsions, if not the disease? Are they abnormal? Should we punish them? What would happen to fixers and spotters who play with the innocent sports enthusiasts' emotions? Should such people be locked-up forever? Understanding these things is my obligation to enlighten a person to know the obsessions of importance, which are essential for our life to continue smoothly in this society. Our country is riddled with orthodoxy but slowly this orthodoxy is getting to redundancy. Taboo does not remain as taboo any more. The people are not tight lipped. People are expressive about their hidden secretes, and hence today's men do not like strait jackets under the social reality constructs. The world does not remain boring. The world is changing, hence, liberalism is a cautious word to be remembered and enforced. Obsessions are there everywhere with all men and women alike. Hence, permission to bet and gamble should be legalised, but fixing and spotting should be punished. There should be knowledge regarding

- ✓ Normal betting and abnormal betting.
- ✓ Effective societal restrictions on bad betting.
- ✓ Police understanding on legalised betting.
- ✓ Political vision on licensing different types of betting.

Considering all these bettings, it should end the evil side of the dirty obsessions and result in useful obsessions in future; if somebody questions me on betting, I personally would answer him "Betting is bad."

Why people bet? I have no answer, but I have an explanation that might not be liked by the people who bet and gamble. Definition of betting and gambling is that,

"Any act or thought where positive energy is absent but tagged only with thrills and negative energy is nothing but betting or gambling."

I do not bother about the Oxford dictionary definitions or explanations on betting and gambling. People want Bollywood clothes and Hollywood suits, because watching both are more thrilling. People want the fast and furious because by driving a car fast, the tangential speed makes a driver experience a thrill of zero gravity. To get this actual experience, we have to hire an aircraft to fly high beyond earth's altitude and ask the pilot to fall free. For this experience, we have to pay a lot of money, for which we are reluctant. Today people are inclined to make immediate money and material. People in a given short time want to make lots of money and stack more materials. While stacking wealth, the thrill is prerogative. People want uninhibited fast sex to experience a thrill but not slow sex, which lacks thrill because usual (so-called normal) sex is a beacon to love. These thrills are like opium, without opium being consumed. The consumption of opium results in arrests by the police under the Consumption of Narcotic Drugs Act, but the thrill does not result in any arrest. Modern man expects higher state of thrill by not consuming narcotics, still he would like to have the required thrill, hence man tries betting and gambling. When people expect to have a drug experience without narcotics, the only way is by betting and gambling. This disease has no treatment except by keeping such people in a high-profile long-stay homes or de-addiction centers. It is for the gambler to choose the traditional spiritual treatment or the high-profile hospital or long-stay managements.

ORAL FIXERS
(To Remember the Freud)

Eventually man cannot escape the wrath of the society, being a part of it. He is always addicted to one or the other items in his march towards death. For example, like getting overly attached to his mother, not addicted to his wife's shopping, entangled in his children's affairs and then finally being permanently a fixture in Lord's abode. This is a usual mundane theory. The stages of fixation are merely an evolutionary process from birth to death. Veda explains the same under "karma" or "*Vidhi*." *Karma* generally means "living process", which is guided by our accounts of the past and is represented as our passbook of credits and debits in our daily banking transactions. In other words, life is our eternal passbook comprising genes. Crediting and debiting are the usual processes of gaining and loosing wealth but the gene passbook helps cleansing our impurities of mind and body or checking the material obsessions. Generally, *Vidhi* is not defined, instead innumerable colourful theories are proposed. I would like to explain *Vidhi* rather than define it:

"It is a remorseful act of escapism by an incompetent intelligent man by which he causes a harmful end to himself and also to others."

This is what I call Oral Fixers. Keeping the Freudian fixing theory apart, it is for the reader to meditate on my explanation. The explanation that I narrate is to highlight smokers. The *Vidhi* always stands for *Kshana* (point), but in this game of smoking, it is a snake and ladder game. Participants in this game are smokers, their spouses, friends, bystanders and doctors who treat them. Actually, Yama is a mute spectator to catch the smoker in this game of hide and seek, waiting for the smokers' *Vidhi*.

"An ignited cigarette stick gets stuck between ones lips, allowing his own lungs to burn and spewing chemicals to cause cancer to a passive smoker is called as Oral Fixing."

Hence, Yama (Lord of Death) is a confused master in this hide and seek drama to catch the true culprit. This is exactly like a *BCCI* chief who cannot decide whether to quit or not when caught in a betting case. If he quits instantaneously, it is good for the game but if he does not quit then the game of cricket suffers. The same concept applies for smokers too. The problem would not be there in the society if they die instantly. This is never the case of smokers, who play running and catching games, which is called *Zoot Aata* (running and catching) for the Lord Yama to catch the elusive smoker. Hence, in this game, the whole social fraternity suffers. The suffering is enormous at the cost of money, and mental and physical health, thus causing institutional downfall. It is good to see that the youth in our country are changing, as awareness about the harmful effects of smoking is increasing. This is because of the persistent effort of non govt orgnisations (NGO's), government, and health departmental awareness programs in our country. The public health system including youngsters' self-awareness programs on their health are improving with antecedent increased on social values. There are approximately hundred chemicals resulting by smoking that can cause cancer for the smoker and there are around thirty odd chemicals that can cause cancer to the passive smoker; but what about industrial pollution? My first quote in my previous book Bend and Mend is about choosing technological neo-industrial progress wherein I have highlighted the psychological health, but in today's environment we are practically spewing chemicals to this wonderful environment by our industries and motor vehicles without effective eco management. What does this mean to us? Should we arrest the industrial minister or should we blame ourselves for our enjoyments. Leftists in our country call true development as conspiracy by the developed countries'; the politicians call the same as their development and the industrialist's call themselves as one who is nurturing employment opportunity to the masses. The sufferer is Mother Nature, and also we the people. Nobody on earth is against development, but not at the cost of the common man. Effective control by the Government, proper scrutiny by bureaucrats, less corruptive practices and many means of innovative technology could prevent a holocaust in future. Let us not blame smoking alone, let us also blame those who do not adopt good disposal mechanisms for our organic waste (garbage). We should also restrain people from burning tires, plastics, rubber and other organic substances, which emits sub-noxious carbon chemicals leading to health hazards. There should be a law to curtail such behaviours by maniacs of a political party or religion. Actually, this amounts to mass smoking, and hence slow mass killing. Thus, we have to put a gag not on the smoker but on those who speak on pollution in their AC chambers because they only talk (oral diarrhea) and never convert them into deeds.

BRAIN THE MADHVA, BRAIN THE RAMANUJA AND BRAIN THE SHANKARAA (My Interpretations are Pertaining to the BRAIN Connectivity)

We all agree that human origin is not from aliens but from our ancestral reptiles as per the evolutionary theory. Our today's intelligence would have survived not because by our present intelligence but from our ancestral instinctual and intellectual assertions. The earlier reptiles had lacked verbal expressions and that is why we now consider ourselves as the hallmark of creation, as humans, because we have good verbal expressions. If by chance they had verbal communication, probably our existence would have not been on this earth. In the earlier days, people who aired their good views on life, mind and matter were actually chased, persecuted and killed by the then rulers (kings and monarchs). The reptile's new brain was like an appendix, which had little function akin to not possessing it. This is the right time for me to make readers aware that in future generations our today's appendix could be a Ripley's collection. This is because the human appendix constantly coming under the surgeon's knife. The gene that encrypts the information for the appendix from one generation to the next would stop doing so as impinging of the appendix marker on gene map would result in losing its ability to decode. Humans evolved after the brain got evolved by the development of forebrain. I call this as 'adding or subtracting phenomenon.' If this my statement is correct, "What next?" Naturally, people imagine their head being vertically added or horizontally subtracted of information. To know and see this arithmetical phenomenon, I have to live millions of years on this earth, which I would not wish. As such, the head is a mystique Pandora Box that houses a more complicated organic mass of neuro-chemico-physico-psycho-spiritual mix.

The brain is an enigma to a scientist and as well as to a spiritualist. The evolutionary answers provide little insight to know and understand the complicated brain. The scientific answer provides few explanations, whereas spiritual understanding provides every explanation of the brain, which people are not ready to accept. This is exactly what had happened to Buddha, whose teachings were not accepted totally in our country. Our country is teaming with a variety of brains; brainy people are always on their toes with "If's" and "But's." Sages visualised the world with "Why's" and "What's." The lord Buddha was free of queries. When his father asked him to be vigilant, he could have thought that he should have been vigilant on enemies from outside. After he attained *Moksha*, he would have realised that the true enemies are within him. His mission was not accomplished as his questions were unanswered because ready answers that were available did not satisfy him. Hence, he himself found the truth, the *Mouna* (silence). His only question was "To whom are we existing?" His answer for this question was categorised into three parts. They are, first to accept, second to realise and third is to move forward. *Adi Shankara Bhashya* has a history of one thousand five hundred years approximately, whereas Buddha's history is three thousand years old. He was the lone sage who called the entire universal phenomenon as educational. Buddha was never disconnected from this world, because if he was disconnected, then he would have failed in his invention of compassionate arsenal to this world.

Our brain to a common observer is split, right and left. Hence, split already exists with different hemispherical functions. As I had already explained, our brain is a most complicated organ of fat and protein with little carbohydrates comparatively and has millions and trillions of neurons well connected through their tracts and centers. Each tract has its own communication system, which would convey signals continuously so as to work and think smoothly. This is like Interpol, which has a well-connected police force in every nook and cranny, spying with bloodhounds. Bloodhound is the only dog that has well equipped Rhinencephalon. We are all weak detectives; hence, our chemistry is limited to lust, whereas dog has fantastic and amazing detective skills and lust is only seasonal in these creatures. Brain is a chemically integrated substance with non-harming organic mass with finites but mind is composed of dispersed non-condensed harmful nascent infinites. Hence, scientifically discovered centers in brain have specific function over body to control self, execute self-functions, to survive and allow to live and let live.

Mac Laren did a lot of work on brain through stimulations and ablations of certain centers to know the exact nature of man's thinking and its executive functions in animals. Hence, for all practical purpose, it is the intactness of brain by neuro-anatomical structures, neuro-bio chemical nature, neuro-physiological functions and neuro-hormonal status that requires for so-called normal functionary of a human or for that matter even for any life to sustain and live. Let me not go into the details of scientific studies conducted on these lines but for the common man's point of view, right brain possess rational thinking and left brain possess logical thinking. The rational thinking in man is always based on language. Proprietary to our responsible thoughts are in the right brain. The rationality invariably is expressed though our verbal medium whereas logics are intuitions. The intuition in humans is always non-verbal. Oration is the quality of rational people. These orators are destined to con and cheat innocents. Therefore, rationality is a weapon to counter political oppositions' jibe or remarks. The person of this character enjoys others oratory weaknesses, whereas an intuitive man is a human with all altruistic humbleness. The altruistic logic of man is always executed to uplift Mother Nature. Political will has made CBI and IB into spineless bodies. Prevalence of suicide in our country is more with scientists when compared to politicians. The basic cause for this could be a weak development of *Brocas* area within the scientist's brain.

Intuitions are not different from delusions. Both of them are out of the blue experiences or experience from nowhere. Delusions are directed on living beings, which becomes paranoid illnesses later. The same delusions on nature are not paranoid illnesses, instead they are intuitions. The odd rationality of a rational person is fear, emotional pain and suffering. The intuitional paranoia has no such sufferings. Intuitive paranoia is always useful to the society and to mankind, like in Newtonian Gravity. Einstein for example had developed a theory of relativity from his intuitive delusion. The theory of relativity at its simplest terms explains that two opposite objects exert electromagnetic force, which can have an effect on the moving objects; hence, the gravity in the universe is not constant due to myriads of such powerful objects in the universe. All that I have explained here is due to the reason that because the universe is woven wonderfully and the bond created is so strong, that which looks seemingly separate as an illusion are really well connected. Brain is no difference when compared to the universe with myriads of sub-nano Milky Ways. Only way to experience this brain is to peep intuitively inside the atomic world. According to neuro-scientists, this Milky Way inside the brain is well connected through neuronal pathways executing their work uninhibited with chemicals but not by electromagnetic forces. Parody is that universal electromagnetic waves have a definite influence on these chemicals present inside the brain, which we see in our changing mood during full moon or no moon days.

Under the Vedanthic terminology, man is a *Purusha* (human being) and he is above all living species, hence *Utthama* (good being).When I consider this didactic view, man could be called as *Purshotthama* (superior being). Let us say if this same being has humbleness or humane touch then he is called as *Maryada Purushotthama* (most respected man). In our past epic stories, we would have seen such a personality in Sri Rama in Ramayana. Hierarchically, man is placed on top of all living species in this world and his brain has been designed by the creator for such a wonderful work that no living species can imagine. These are "Reasoning, Analysis and Execution." Generally, all these functions are included in one domain called as the cognitive function. We are on top because of two functions that we possess. They are the creativity and the skill. The root of these functions lies in the right brain and the left brain, respectively. Hence, what brings both halves together? These functions are brought out so smoothly by the interaction of left and right brains with central corpus callosum. To the periphery of corpus callosum lies the limbic system, which controls our basic functions; they are the thoughts, the procreation and the emotions. Our thoughts are executed by our actions through sensory neuronal spino-thalamico-cerebral tracts and balanced through the auro-cerebro cerebellar tracts along with visuo-spino-auro cerebellar tracts. The harmonious or our servo-mechanism has been taken care by baro-neuro-humoral secretions. Self-body esteems are being managed by numerous neuronal plexus distributed in our neck, thorax, abdomen and pelvis. This is exactly the reason why I call *Madhwa (Dwaitha)* the brain because we have two independent brains, I call *Ramanuja (Vishista Adhwaitha)* the brain because of various paths and tracts, and I call *Shankaraa (Adhwiatha)* the brain because middle brain or old limbic system is one which takes care of all the functions of brain and the body.

LANGUAGE BUSTERS (The Boastfulness)

The most perplexing human interactive business is through our language. In our evolutionary process, whatever the refined or change that had taken place since ages is in the language. This language has united and as well as destroyed the human race. The language is the unit to bind the humans and thus create innumerable and various sects and religions. The pre-supposed and pre-proposed nouns, adjectives and metaphors in our Lexicon of language have taken hundreds of defeats from the intelligent hammer before it went for a mold to ultimate regular use by the human race. There is no doubt that one's language is a comfortable dose provider to cure members belonging to a particular sect or religion when they are living in groups in an alien language state or living in groups far away. There were arguments and counter arguments in building the efficient anatomy of language and in this process many philosophers were executed by rightists and leftists of the monarchs in that period. The language bears the brunt of inheritance and also language depends on the neuro-structural development.

In my practice, I have observed that invariably the first child generally has dyslexia in its various expressional capacities. When I ponder and observe our ancient Hindu undivided Family (HUF) divisionary techniques, when children opt for their family material division, it was in vogue for the first male child to inherit two portions of wealth, for example, if there were four male children, the division would be five equal portions including the father's part. Though I am not an expert in HUF laws, I suppose that by succession the only son of any family would inherit his entire father's possession automatically. Hence, in Hindu undivided family, the eldest son of his many male siblings would get one portion more. It baffled me a little bit for this indifference. I tried to find the reasons for this indifference among brothers, which I could not get in any of the old scriptures. When I enquired few Pundits and Scholars, I failed to get a suitable answer from them. I scratched my head, I struggled a lot and took time to think before coming to a possible reason behind such a division or the reason for this indifference. I might be wrong in explaining; still I would like to share.

We are all from the mystique organic Pandora Box, our mother's uterus. Our evolution was based on opposite sex and their chemistry, the appropriate mix of chemicals, neo-chemical organisations and its process of organic production inside the box with a suitable platform for the foetus or progeny to grow. This is akin to a party or function where with various materials like bench, stool, light, sound system and electricity, we could draw the décor of this party or function. Initially, to organise an event by an immature organiser is a big task. But, he could complete this function with little faults here and there. The same function to be organised by an experienced event manager is very easy. Here I am left with confusion whether experience works or knowledge. There is a saying that each organ in our body is like a human with intelligence. So, we can say that each cell is a human. As man has to get adopted in the society for his fruitful life, so also the cell has to get adapted to the environment inside the body. It is acronymic to say that our gastro-intestinal tract (GIT) today is adapted well for poisonous pesticides, which the farmers would use for their agricultural products. If this dictum is true, uterus too should get adapted. I remember reading some articles regarding abortion of the first conception in late East Germany, which was legalised by the then Government in that country. The reason that I am going to explain might leave little confusion to the reader. According to me, the first conceived uterus fails to furnish necessary nutrients to the foetus, especially for neuro-nodal development of the foetus. The reason is said to be ill-developed vascular openings between the placenta and the myo-metrium at first instance of a conception. Hence, mother would have failed to provide good nourishment, especially the B-Complex, which is an important factor in the good development of an embryonic brain. Thus, there could be a brain abuse, which is not in the form of trauma or disease but an iota of damage in the form of neuro-physio-chemical development of certain centers and tracts, which are necessary for the arithmetic capability and also for the proper development of certain centers pertaining to comprehension and expression of lexicons of language. Such children have been labeled as tube light by their teachers, when these children were sent to school. Basically, they are slow learners and if they are focused and are shown *Anubhuthi* (little warmth) by teachers, they would excel well in their education. For all said and done, the language is not our whole and sole property, hence we need not have a proprietary tag or value to the language. What does this mean to our languages? What language busting is about? I have a narration on this.

We have ghost busters who are hired to drive out invisible ghosts to get relieved from the nuisance they create in our mind or for our paranoia and hallucinations. I too have in my place such ghost busters and sorcery makers. In Kannada language, the same phenomenon is called as *Maata Manthra* (sorcery), in which people go to a meat-eating goddess to get relieved from the sorcery done on them by imagined or known people. This is called *Thade Hodeyodu* (where a small mud pot is used with egg and sometime with an animal {hen, sheep, goat or buffalo} sacrifice to the goddess after certain rituals. These rituals have some *Thanthric* fervour performed only by certain people). Language busters are exactly opposite of this where they bust the inappropriate words, metaphors, adjectives and nouns of others and keep hammering them with their armoury of language. The ghost busters' work is to remove fear of the people but language busters' work is to induce unnecessary fear in the people. Language is innate in our genes, which expresses through *Udgaetha* or *Prana* (air) in congruent cues from the world and also by the thought of a person. The language busters are otherwise known as Fault Seekers. The language cannot perfect a man. The man may be perfect in his language but to be a human he would require perfectness in his mind and the use of language should coincide or be congruent between these two phenomena. If any human possesses this asset, then he is not a language buster. He is actually a language enhancer. The *Kara* (chilly) mixture is always tasty so also the mixture of language (Kanglish) and mixture of deeds (different good works). The language busters are those who comment on our innate faulty vocabulary process, for example, *Gate Bagilu;* the *Bagilu* is a gate in Kannada language and the same gate is being used in

English meanwhile. Hence, this is also a different mixture. People should be magnanimous to taste such mixtures. While talking with one of my friend I used a casual word like '*Ondu Thara* (a sort of)', which he felt was half-derogatory to his personality. Matters reached a boiling point, and was about to explode. In our life, do we need such meritorious qualities of language to live? Such qualities of a person would be an example to crash with no remedy. No man is there on the earth who masters everything; hence, language also falls into this category. After all, language is necessary for a man to communicate and express. When I came out from mother's womb, I was nothing. I had no name except form. My name is arbitrary and I have my name only for the identification purpose. Hence, I should not think on proprietary rights of my ego because the proprietorship holds good for the business. I am not in this world for pure business, I am here for my good business to hold on to the society. The business I am talking should possess dispersing quality to bring the society together. When I expressed this statement to my friend, he had a skewed glee, for which I did not show any botheration.

GARUDA KAMBA (The Temple Pillar)

A boy, who was aged 16 years, studying in 10th standard, had come with his mother for counselling. His mother was a lecturer in biology; she had only one son, hence automatically had concurrent possessiveness. Her expressional possessiveness was so big that all her deficiencies would be transferred onto her son. His father was working in a private company; he was well poised and quite understanding. The Mother was dull in mathematics due to non-conceptualisation of arithmetical symbols; hence, she was having dyscalculia in her school days. As she was so much obsessed about her earlier scholastic weaknesses in mathematics, she would expect hundred percent results from her only son in mathematics. She, being a biology lecturer, failed to realise her son's problem with mild dyscalculia. She would always insist her son to come first in school. She was very critical of her son. He should not have played outside more than the stipulated time prescribed by his mother; he should not mix with his friends very often; she always expected him to study and kept teaching perfectionism in all subjects except biology. It was natural for her son to hate her for her extraordinary watchful eyes on him. It was a typical mother and son bondage (loving overtly and hating covertly). This behaviour of his mother changed him to become more and more sensitive *(Bhavanthmaka)*. He had felt many times that: why should he read? What then after reading? This son who was losing slowly his mother's warmth gradually began seeking the same with the opposite sex, a classmate. This odd behaviour of him had made his mother to bring him for counselling. In my counselling sessions, I had answered many finer aspects of their relationships. After which, he got relieved of his few problems and also I explained to his mother regarding the emotional positive attachments. I asked his mother to have a macro view rather than a micro view about her son. Probably, my counselling would have helped him to overcome his emotional problems. For his inattentiveness and irritability, I had prescribed him mild antidepressants from which he did respond well, which was evident in his subsequent follow-ups.

Interestingly he was wearing a full arm T-shirt with an eagle picture print on the left side of the T-shirt. I got curious about the print and I questioned him "For what does Eagle in your T-shirt stands for?" The answer from him was "I don't know"; his mother too replied the same. Both of them left my chamber after acknowledging my counselling session. The *Garuda* picture on his T-shirt and *Garuda sthamba* in our Hindu temples really baffled me and I tried to figure out few answers to it. I got amazed to find few of my own concepts on *Garuda Sthamba.* It is my interpretation, I might be wrong in my explanation. As per my memory, in my childhood days, when I was visiting many great and famous temples with my family, I used to ask uncomfortable questions to my late grandfather, ", *Thatha* (grandfather), why this *Garuda* (eagle) idol is present?" When we enter many big temples, we would have observed *Garuda* idols lying idle before we reach Sanctum Sanctorum of the important deities. My grandfather would give vivid answers to my innocent questions. He told these idols are meant for *Garudothsawa* (a ritual performed on the deity sitting over the eagle). I was too young to understand all his explanations. Today, the concepts of Eagle or *Garuda* as logo have some real social bearings and throw meaning to life in some of the countries. In the bird kingdom, Eagle is considered as the King. Its telescopic eyes are meant for 'good vision.' This is meant for Eagles' survival, but in our temples why does the Eagle idol exist? Probably I feel that the eagle statue in our temples has some hidden or symbolic meanings, as per our Hindu Mythology. Presence of telescopic vision for a high flying eagle allows it to find its prey on the surface easily. The country can never prosper if the caretaker of that nation does not possess far vision for his nation's development. In this vision of development, the chief of that nation should possess three 'S.' These are the Scale, Strategy and Speed. This great bird possesses all these qualities. Scale is the distance, next is the spatial strategy of catching the prey and last is the speed by which the bird attacks its prey. In our national development, they are the following:

- ✓ Scale of the works.
- ✓ Strategy of works.
- ✓ Speed of the works.

These are the three basic principles. All these three points are added advantage to our Gross Developmental Product (GDP) growth. The job created by such an activity is a sure income to the common tax-paying man. Being a psychiatrist, sometimes I think that at what cost this development would bring harmony, peace and mental health. I feel money and matter would not bring all the necessary tranquility. Therefore, if peace and development both develop simultaneously, I think we could have a good socio-psychological economic progress.

Coming to *Garuda* (eagle) and its *Sthamba* (stone pole) or *Kamba* in our temples, there could be some mystical symbolic meanings behind such ritualistic architectural marvels. The God we all know as omnipresent or *Sarvanthrayami* does not require any temple. The concept of temple is meant only for us to seek happiness or to get relieved from stress. The worship places are constructed across the world on faith and belief. Truly speaking I do not know this faith and belief because as a psychiatrist I believe only mind. Solace is actually a mind state. This state one could get without a temple. If somebody says faith and belief are the two states of mind, I would like to advise them to possess 'faith' to alleviate pain (anxiety) and 'belief' to believe himself as a human (humbleness).

Today temples are too busy in collecting material and money rather than imbibing moral standards to the people who visit. It is neither temples nor God's problem, it is our problem of genetically inherited idiocy. Today, the mute God sitting inside the temple's Sanctum Sanctorum and the people surrounding this mute God are busy in collecting our offerings. I feel symbolically that He simply looks at us (if at all he has vision) when we visit the temples but He is unable to see the poor people who cannot visit Him. It was thought earlier by the temple *Vasthu* experts after constructing big temples that God should have a periscope because he cannot view the world clearly, as his Sanctum Sanctorum always gets choked by the rich visitors visiting Him. Therefore, the architects in those days erected these *Sthambas* (pole) as *Garuda Kambas* (eagle stone poles) in front of the core seat of God. Symbolically, it means to me that by this eagle pole, God can view the distant world habitations like sailors in a submarine who could view the happenings above the water sitting inside their submarines through their periscope. By analysing or having logic behind such constructions, I came to a conclusion that the God we speak of has fantastic vision of compassion and imparts good to the people, irrespective of their religion, cast, creed, rich or poor and those who visit Him or those who do not. However, we have failed in our effort to carry these benefits to the poor or downtrodden faraway because we have converted our Gods into the commercial iconic blind idols.

COLOUR TERRORISM
(No Remedy in the Near Future)

People are afraid or scared of colours today. Each colour has a particular significance. In a multiethnic and multi-religious country like ours, religion, love, *LGBT* (Lesbian, Gay, Bisexual and Transgender) and some diseases like *AIDS* are all identified by their own individual colour logos. Each group or organisation has been identified and discriminated by their colours. Present-day politicians with such political colour overtones have utilised these colour logos effectively for their dirty antisocial music. Hence, a common man in our country suffers by seditious activity colluding with the associated favourable religious colours. When we love *VIBGYOR* and appreciate nature's charm, we are so mean to identify and heartily love the same colours individually. Thus, we fail in bringing religious and ethnic harmony. I have already explained our tricolour as a symbol of life rather than religious equality in my first book *Parivarthana* (the change). It is fine under our *Samvidhan* (constitution) today, but this affair would require an urgent relook or there should be an amendment for betterment of our future generations to enjoy one colour. This amendment might not be a possibility in the near future because colour division is a pre-requisite for our politicians to hold on to their (politicians) chairs. This amendment could be a possibility for each individual if we try to understand our own families.

I am a psychiatrist. I understand my own family and my clients' families who come for counselling. Before I come to this real issue, let me explain an interesting story in my own family. My mother-in-law who is a witty, intelligent old woman is fond of sari colours, which youngsters would invariably prefer. I was thrilled to know the demand by my mother-in-law who had asked her daughter to purchase a saree having oceanic blue or oil blue colour sari. Frankly, I am very poor in identifying new colours. After hearing from my wife, I felt that this is the time for me to unofficially fix a colour logo for two different socio-family structures. They are the "Occupants" and the "Intruders." Hence, "Marine blue" is for the "Occupants" family, which is an existing structure, and the "Oil blue" is for the "Intruders", who actually migrate from another family structure. To my surprise, the 'blue' in these two colours is the common colour. Interestingly, I do not want to relate these two colours to our environmental disasters? To safeguard the marine life and fauna, it is an arduous task to the mariners to cleanse the oil sleek, which would have occurred accidentally by the ships carrying oil tanks. Everyone knows that this is one of the many manmade environmental disasters. Whenever or wherever there is an oil sleek, mariners are asked to clean the same. Exactly in the similar fashion, occupants of a family are asked by the intruder from another family to work. Leave aside the environmental disasters because these disasters could have been prevented only by the grace of God, the similar cognizance of disaster could be managed well in a family with better understanding by the individuals involved. Here, the "Occupants" are the occupants of a particular family, a self-explanatory word, and the "Intruder" is a person coming from another family, example a 'daughter-in-law.'

How does difference of opinion arise? Let me explain with my limited knowledge. The outside signals perceived would get processed in the brain and the information what we get out from the analysis of such signals should have a highest expressional value or quality. This never happens in majority of the marriages. The bonding advantage invariably breaks. Probably this could happen mainly by "Alchemy", a chemical acceptance. How could we solve this major basic indifference? I have tried a model. This model of my management is possible only for those who are trained to accept. In a family, there is already an occupant (mother). The mother's job is to allow a legal intruder (daughter-in-law). Hence, all over the world, the intruder should be accommodated by the occupant. By meditating on this statement and with a deep understanding of the underlying phenomenon, let me go into the larger issue.

We are endowed with sufficient knowledge to rule the whole world. We were having many *Sages, Manus* and *Altruistics*. All of them are confined to our limited world. They never tried to find or discover the outside world other than theirs. Meanwhile, our country was discovered by explorers like Vasco da Gama. After this discovery, our business or trade with other nations and our nation improved significantly. Our country prospered with wealth and also with income (until the British landed on our land). Hence, people from abroad loved our country and decided to settle permanently here. Most importantly, the Hindu Rajas and Maharajas of ester days probably might have not sensed the scale of present disharmony (from Mughal's and British's rule). The reason would be that from ages we have developed a sincere hospitality attitude, which is deeply inherited in our genes. As per our customs, regularly in our *Pooja* (offering) rituals we always invoke Lord Ganesha first and offer him what a guest would be offered by our ritualistic symbolic gestures. In Veda, the same is termed as the *Sathkara Bhaava* (guest feeling) or the *Athithi Devo Bhava* (to take care of the guest as God). Our erstwhile *Maharajas* allowed all intruders inside our country and looked after them well. This was done probably by the then Kings to strengthen their power, to appoint them as soldiers, to fight their enemies, to employ them to work in their field or for some other type of benefits. These intruders grew, prospered and lived happily.

I am basically a human and I humbly accept all intruders. What I want to convey subtly (*Sukshma*) is that a difference of opinion with occupant and intruder makes all the difference to accept the colour or not which I have previously mentioned. A small bean of hate would have led to a deep religious division today. Therefore, this difference has gone to such a propensity where even God cannot handle this deep-rooted disease of hate among us. *Manus* with recent political clout failed to bridge the deep wide crack of hate, which is been created by the saffron colour, the green colour and also by the white colour. It has grown beyond our repair. The worrying part is to find the suitable adhesives, the *Athma Chinthana* (self-realisation) and the *Sadbhavana* (feeling of oneness), to patch different poles as one. The patching gels I see are:

- ✓ To provide proper education.
- ✓ To create more and more jobs.
- ✓ By increasing our socio-economic status.
- ✓ Building oneness among individuals.

Some of our *Buddi Jeevis* (intelligentsia) hold our whole nation to ransom. Fine, ours is a democratic country. Given a chance, I would love to be a democrat. Frankly speaking, the democracy have been hijacked and laid to rest in a pseudo-secularist graveyard. Being a psychiatrist, I am able to counsel the grieved party, but in a country like ours the referendum only would bring a change. Techniques of appeasement to a particular religion and freebies to a particular class of society do not work economically in the long run and our deep understanding of who is an intruder and who is an occupant helps our present irreparable problems. The intruder's hard work to the motherland and efficient soul search by the occupant to accommodate are the only solutions present that I could think of. In other words, it is basically a confidence-building exercise by the occupants. The acceptance of an intruder by an occupant is humanity; meanwhile, accepting rituals and customs of an occupant by the intruder is also humanity. Finally, the largesse of millions of hearts necessitates binding the different colours of any country, which matters most for total harmony; that is why the natural *VIBGYOR* colours look wonderful to me.

SOCIAL ATOM BOMB (A Word SADHBHAVANA to Meditate on)

The Lord Buddha had said 'we are all one; everything is one.' He had come to this simple conclusion from practicing deep meditation. Many feel that meditation is done by closing one's eyes. To fresh up of our idea of meditation, let me explain that Lord Buddha never closed his eyes while performing his meditation. People would wonder how this could be possible. I have explained Open Meditation in my first book Parivarthana (the change) under the concept of Complicated Tap in detail. I explain extensively the same subject in my next book Praarthana (the prayers).

Let me share my experience. When I was doing my Diploma in Psychiatry, I was subjected to undergo auto-biofeedback to test my concentration by a friend of mine, who was an M Phil Neuro-psychology trainee. I accepted the same on her request. This machine was new to her department. Her thesis work assigned was based on auto-biofeedback studies. She was smart, nice and very friendly. She had asked me to come in the morning for her test thinking that my attention would be more during morning hours. She took a lot of care while putting the paste and the electrodes on my head. She explained how her machine works and how this test helps in her thesis. When a man relaxes and closes his eyes, the alpha brain waves would increase in quantity. This machine picks up these alpha wave signals and feeds them to the computer. After computing the alpha waves, the machine converts the alpha brain waves into a visual mode or into a music form so that person under relaxation with closed eyes would hear the music or with his eyes open he would see the red light. This is how this machine would allow an anxious man to self-relax more and more. Here, according to her, the relaxation obtained was like a sort of meditation. She asked me to relax and close my eyes. To her surprise, I could hear no music, or when my eyes opened, I did not even see the red light. She felt sorry about me because she would have thought I am a useless man. According to her, to become knowledgeable, a person has to concentrate more and should possess high degree of attention. Frankly, the reason why I was unable to concentrate was whenever I was closing my eyes I would only imagine the beautiful image of her. Let me put the event in a simple way, when I was closing my eyes, I would have her in my mind with lusty (sorry to her) thoughts. When I was not closing my eyes, I perceived her as a friend. In friendship, unclean feeling would not arise. For all practical purposes, while we open our eyes, the alpha waves would respond to the visual stimuli, thus losing all its character or its eight to nine Hertz thirty to forty micro-volts *PC* (Pereito Occipital) dominant activity. This is how alpha brain waves could get disturbed. Hence, computer was not at all picking up my scanty alpha waves, which could come in the form of music or in the form of red light. If lust was the true factor, how could I relax with my closed eyes? How could I express my feelings to her? This is exactly the reason why Lord Buddha asked us to meditate with our eyes open. Now, I feel that we should learn the art of developing good amounts of alpha waves with our eyes wide open contrary to the existing rule that opening eyes would obliterate alpha waves generated in the mind when eyes are closed. For this novel technique, I named the same as 'Open Meditation.'

Lord Buddha while meditating arrived at a fascinating, fabulous and amazing conclusion regarding the 'Sphere" scene of *Brahman* (universe). Some argued that the same teaching by Buddha was known as *Shoonya* philosophy. How could he arrive to this conclusion? This was possible by his pure meditation with eyes open. While he was in deep meditation under a banyan tree, there were some occasions when he could view the *Brahman* up, as leaves of banyan tree breezed sidewards. After observing the *Brahman*, he was of the opinion that he is sitting under a mammoth enclosed umbrella with its penumbra. This half umbrella, which he meditated on, has an infinite height and also infinite either sides. He also viewed another half of this inverted umbrella, down under him. To this phenomenon or conclusion he could have arrived possibly after observing a washer man wash his linen. He was of the opinion that infinite down under meets the infinite back, then infinite up to infinite front and back to infinite down under. This is what *Shoonya* is all about. The same was renamed by Sage Aryabhatt as zero. Without zero, crores would not have been present today. In mathematical world, zero is everything. This digit ends where it started. Hence, it is a continuous process. No other symbol in arithmetic has a continuous flow. Every other digit has to end somewhere, if not, this digit possess no meaning at all. When Lord Buddha meditatively soldered both umbrellas, he found a huge spherical ball housing all living and non-living things inside the infinite circle. After viewing the true nature of different lives and materials, he had proclaimed *"We are all one."* He never ended his ideas here. His meditation was so deep; he went on into the depth of the matter. He came to the conclusion that when *Brahman* is spherical, the tiniest part of the matter should also be spherical in nature. The present-day atomists would agree that what Lord Buddha said was correct. The atomist is one who gets tucked inside the atom and views its wonderful world when compared to atoms' size. Further, Lord Buddha concluded that living and non-living things bind by an invisible, pervading and strong energising particle, which is elusive, elementary and God like. Even today, we are experimenting to find such a particle called Higgs Boson or Gods Particle in our large and most expensive laboratories. Still, we are futile in searching the elusive particle. Let us hope that one day we would find such a particle. We also should hope that the discovery of such a particle would unite this whole world into one.

After deep meditation by Lord Buddha, he viewed life comprising of sorrows and happiness as a perfect acrimony of opposites. They are situated between two infinite ends and in the center *Brahman*, who is sitting, is our consciousness. From his enlightened thought, he found that *Brahman* (cosmos) is in spherical form. The atom he viewed was also round shaped, so also the womb in a woman; then the society we much talk about should also possess circles charged with energy. In English literature, we say, 'in your circle', we never say, 'in your square.' Similarly, Lord Buddha confirmed this analogy of social circles, which I christened as the 'Social Atom." These social atoms are Mini *Brahmans* when they are compared to the existing material atom. The same social atom is a speck or a subatomic particle in front of this *Brahman*. When we artificially subject material atoms to friction, it would release enormous energy. Similarly, when man moves from one social atom to another social atom, as just narrated, it would produce psychological friction, a negative energy. Atomic energy we obtain from such friction has many useful functions like the production of electricity and the same can be used as atom bombs to destroy humankind. One is construction and another is destruction, a dual nature of energy is explained here. The energy released by the friction of social atoms would cause 'destruction' by 'hate.' The destruction caused by nuclear fission can be re-constructed by money and material but the hatred that arises by the social friction cannot be cooled so easily. In our present society, politics, judiciary, parliament affairs, police, etc. are trying to extinguish hate from people's mind. All of us have failed miserably in order to harmonise the various minds because 'hate' would remain in dormant state with such social circles comprising religious groups. The harmony is possible when there is a deep understanding of their minds by haters. What social atom means to me?

Removal of sorrow in our life would not balance the umbrella of life. Lord Buddha called sorrow as *Chintha* (worry); he advocated a simple solution for this problem as *Achintha* (*Shoka* to *Ashoka* or no worry). To live in the above-mentioned sphere, both are pre-requisites. With one, we cannot complete a circle. Till now, I was explaining Buddhism and Materialism. Now coming to the point what the social atom is all about, when we talk much about the 'worry' and the 'sorrow', we tend to create more and more social atom bombs. The mega universe is represented with spherical expansion from a point of its source, so also the structure of an atom around a nucleus. For the science, said explanations are fine but what I mean about this social atom is quite interesting to the reader. In this world, deteriorating faith, paranoiac belief, depleting knowledge, narrow thinking, lack of understanding, lack of acceptance and many such other social issues are because of this said social atom bomb, which we would not trigger to explode, but this bomb is only to feel what has eroding effects on our minds. The feel of this horrific change left us to worry. The very idea to an innocent man of people carousing at swanky hotels with all ill earned money drives him to a state of despondency, depression and suicide. If we want to call this phenomenon in simple terms as 'crumbling society', yes it is a correct word from my side. If this is the present situation in our society, any view of a practicing psychiatrist on the psyche of a population should be broadly based.

Generally, depression is being classified into mild, moderate and severe for treatment purposes. In my view, the mild depression should not be managed, it should be left alone. According to the new Diagnostic and Statistical Manual (DSM) classifications of mental disorders, the common coughs and colds of our psyche are been mentioned as major mental disorders and treated accordingly. As per the new *DSM* classification on mental disorders, no man on the earth can escape the psychiatrist's wrath. I am sure that the anti-psychiatry chorus increases all over the world if this tendency of classification and terminologies continues in the field of psychiatry. Institutional agencies, law abiders and politicians have to look into these matters, not me. Let me explain what this social atom bomb means to our life or to our society in general.

Who is normal or abnormal? Let us not argue on these lines of idealism versus materialism. The same analogy holds similar to what philosophers argue, whether life came first or matter. For me this 'abnormal' looks very much against the snug (cozy) environment; hence, let me discuss on this issue. I already explained the universe being spherical, so also the said society is been positioned and tucked into various bunches of concentric circles. So, our society is strong by way of binding with these innumerable circles. The reason for the elements to bind strongly is because of their physical property, but in the case of people, it is the people's comforts. The cozy attitude of these people binding them firmly inside such circular zones is probably the supposed reason I find. People of all classes in a society keep moving to and fro between these circles, where penetration to these different zones would require huge energy from an individual belonging to one zone. While passing the imaginary borders of these innumerable zones, any identified person would encounter all dysphoria and fear psychosis. Hence, to remain, not to remain in these different circles, depends on the acceptance of individuals belonging to such circles and finding different ways to lead a good life even though staying there would cause difficulties. If we look carefully into the atom, it has high resolution and is very dynamic; so also are the societal atoms revolutionary and moving. Interesting to note is that I am considered as normal by my friend, my relative or by someone of my own circle; but when I move to another circle, which is lower to my status or above my status, I am considered as abnormal by that circle where I enter into. This is exactly why I call society is connected strongly with innumerable or infinite concentric circles with strong borders. This statement of mine looks like a parody for the reader. Practically, to be connected, we all think that there should be a smooth flow between one society to another society with love and affection. Here, in our society, it is opposite, which is working but still connected strongly. A physicist would throw a light on this phenomenon. He would agree that when subatomic particles are more fast and furious in an atom, then the binding capacity of that element is very strong. The very culture of our society, our different languages, performing different rituals, huge socio-economical gaps in us, the educational standards we have, peoples' knowledgeable skills and our basic mind sets have made a dent to prevent living together in one circle. People mixing, talking, sharing and thinking with each one of them has made a person alien when he tries to enter inside the various circles.

Acceptance and realisation makes a social atom bomb to implode but invariably we see explosions by the revolutionary fanatics. This is because of non-acceptance and non-realisation. This can be solved if all of us have one *Bhavana* (feeling), the compassion or the forgiveness. Hence, urgent need of uniting these circles is a necessity to call ourselves as the number one democratic country of this world. For this to be achieved, *Sadhbhaavana* is the only answer at present that I could think of. The atoms of a diamond bind the diamond strong and it shines. If this binding gets detached by mere application of heat or extreme cold, then this diamond loses its lustre. Similarly, our societal strong bondage keeps detaching by the appeasement, by favouring and spewing venoms by different religious ethnic circles but not by the application of heat or cold. If these negative social issues keep increasing, one day, we all will explode into smoke or into gas, which vanishes in thin air. This is what the social atom bomb means to me.

THREE MUSKETEERS OF DEATH (Athos, Aramis, Prothos and NACHIKETHA)

These three above-mentioned men are known heroes to the people of France when French people's lives were in jeopardy. In our Hindu culture too we have such great characters to control the demons. In our epic Mahabaratha, Arjuna was named after *Madhu* for the simple reason that he killed the demon *Madhukeshwara.* We have Gods and Goddesses who possess weapons in their hands, only to convey to the people their intolerance towards mischievous, rowdy and dangerous elements in the society. Adi Shankara Charya called a *Purush* as *Aham Brahmasmi,* who possesses both God and Demon within him. He used this phrase for God killing the Demon or to kill the negativity by the positivity within. If this is the true story then there should not be any controversy regarding Indian mythological Gods or Goddesses iconographies possessing weapons in their hands. There are innumerable comic characters from Chota Bheema to Phantom, including Zoro, Superman or Spiderman, who meant to destroy societal evils. Hence, why are only Indian mythological icons targeted? We do observe the same with European or with Greek mythological icons. They too hold weapons in their hands to safeguard the world from evil. According to me, Jesus is like a *Maha Rushi.* When the sage is termed as God, why not Jesus? Different groups of Christians do not believe Jesus as God, he is only the messenger. Messengers who carry peace do not carry weapons along with them. Truly, Rama or Krishna are not Gods, they are messengers of goodness to the people. They never carried their weapons always with them but used their weapon judiciously only when there was a social anarchy or a war. The creator is the God; hence, Hindus called the omniscient (creator) as God (Lord Shiva), and when the Spirit is God for somebody, similarly something may be God for someone.

My friend was recouping at his home after a brief period of illness. It was my courtesy to visit him in order to enquire his health at his residence. While we were served tea, a friend of his came dashing towards my friend with an inquisitive look and also with a loud voice, which created ripples in the room. It was like a '*Kampana* (earth tremors)' feeling. This friend of his is not a close friend; his antics of this proportion were not called for. What my friend wanted was just an "*Anukampa* (nano *Bhavana*)." This is exactly what happens when someone express all their feelings loudly to others. In fact, they are not honest to their friends. They appear superficially full of emotions but inside they are shallow.

While I was talking with my friend, another friend of her's came and expressed her anguish regarding her relative's daughter who had done her tenth standard well, but in her PUC first year she did her exams badly because she was diagnosed with renal failure. The poor family members got all investigations done on her and they even tried for a renal transplant but somehow nothing was successful. She was on the verge of death. This friend of my friend was narrating the scenes after her visit to this patient, it was a heart-rendering story. We all dispersed, but at night, this patient kept coming in my thoughts like an imaginary movie. The pictures of her total innocence, pleading eyes, crippled and bloated body, wet cheeks, crying mother, helpless father and 'let us try' attitude by the treating doctor, who was showing optimism in a negative atmosphere, kept coming to my mind. This pseudo-optimism is a real problem with many of our doctors who hide the medical facts and ultimately get beaten up by the bystanders. I feel doctors should deliver promptly the facts about the illness to patients and to the patient's well-wishers. Hiding facts might lead to legal problems later. I remember my beloved professor had reminded me and had encouraged to practice transparent psychiatry in relation to my consciousness and context. This girl's innocent question kept on repeating in my mind "Mummy, what was the fault in me to suffer like this?" What answer could the mother give? To explain frankly, I do not have any answer for her. The halcyon days of her youth, the balmy time she would have thought to spend, the castles she would have constructed, the blossom of her youth she would have experienced, the colours she would have thought of enjoying, the aspirations which she wanted to accomplish, all were dealt harshly by Lord Yama. When we focus on her innocent mind, which was destined to be lit by the *Prathibha* (knowledge), suddenly the fate pushed her into darkness. How could anybody console her? Blaming God would do any better for her? When I was discussing with one of my friend, he labeled this tragedy as 'vidhi', which I totally rebut, it is only harsh reality, which one has to accept. For God it is fine to take an innocent adolescent's life because he wanted only good people with him. Meditating at the propensity to be split here between the kind and pure mind and the impure and rotten body, those who call themselves fit and strong on earth are not wise minded. The world would be better if wise minds are present in sound bodies. This happens only with few. I plead to God, if at all He exists. Then 'let there be a transformation from good to wise for a better and best society.' This story is the first Musketeer of death, the Athos.

My friends hired a luxury bus to attend a medical conference at far off coastal city. All my friends felt that journey by night would be pleasant. The bus they had hired was a higher-end version; hence, my travelling friends were sure of their safe journey. However, accident is an accident. While the bus was cruising smoothly in the highway around midnight, probably the drivers fault, the bus went wayside after colliding with the rear end of a parked mini lorry. The lorry, which had collided with their luxury bus, took a sky route to collide with another SUV, which was parked on the side service road. In this fateful night of chain accidents, three *Ayyappa* (famous deity for millions of people across the country) devotees, who were sleeping on the service road by the side of their parked vehicle, died on the spot. The driver of the luxury bus too died on the spot. My friends returned with minor injuries and a few friends, who had fractured their bones, were medically assisted at a nearby city hospital. My wife and I went to the hospital where my friends were recovering from their injuries. A slightly injured friend of mine was narrating the dark side of the event like a movie to both of us; meanwhile, he felt sorry and also expressed his helplessness to a survived girl's innocent question, who was actually a daughter to one of the pilgrims who had died. It was a heart-rending experience. He was explaining his inability to render medical services to a dead body when he was asked by the deceased pilgrim's daughter to bring her father back. He said, "I was speechless. She was pleading her innocence; she held my feet requesting, 'you say you are a doctor. Save my papa?' She was a witness to her father's death. Death has no mercy on us and death is certain, but a sensible death could be a mere postponement. Death does not spare anybody; it is in any moment of time that death would conquer us. Death does not differentiate the poor from the rich; death does not appease different religions, death does not allow any intelligent person to live for two hundred years, neither does it spare a wise man with credentials, who would have had possessed values and virtues in his life. Frankly, the previously mentioned values and virtues would not allow a man to be a martyr. Yes, by means of pure understanding and realisation, death could be postponed. This is possible by way of adopting the meditating techniques available. God has bestowed his mercy on us to conquer death every night by *Kshana Nidhra* (deep sleep) not *Chira Nidhra* (death). Should we not thank God for his mesmerising wakefulness every day, until permanently we succumb to the *Chira Nidhra*? The first symptom of any mental disorder is sleeplessness. The psychiatrist's wealth is dependent on the management of this sleeplessness effectively. Hence, man always yearns for micro deaths. The parody of death is that the man is always scared of his death but still he loves to have temporary deaths. Here also the psychiatrist's wealth doubles because he manages the obsession of death too. Aptly, I would call this as double *Dhamaka* (double earning). No man could possess balanced mind if he has no sleep. There are many vital roles and functions to play by sleep that helps in retaining the prudence of a man. Details regarding the role of sleep on mind equilibrium are available in any psychiatry textbook to an inquisitive reader.

While reading *Katha Upanishath* I was interested, in three *Suthras* –

Isro Ritir Yad Avasir Grihya Ma Asana
Brahman Athithe Namasya,

Namasthithou Brahmanan Avasthi Meshu Asmath
Prathi Threm Vara Vrinasya.

In this *Suthra,* aged Nachiketha's father was distressed as he was reaching nearer to his death. He was harbouring obsession of death. To postpone his death, he wanted to offer his weak cows and earned non-required materials to *Brahmin*, which was confused by his son Nachiketha by differing on his father's obeisance. The father had lost his patience for his son's frequently asked doubts, "Father, would such offerings protect you from death, why do you offer weak cows and materials from which this *Brahmin* cannot earn or use our material; if you think of offering, kindly offer me, I may be a useful to *Brahmin*? " His father *Vajraasa* could not answer his son's doubts, as he was deluded with only fear of his death and thoughts of possessing powers from such offerings. Innocent Nachiketha in that tender age wanted to know only the truth. He was not having any malicious intentions to snub his father. Accidentally or willingly, under a delirious state, the father suggested his son to the *Brahmin* as an offering instead of his weak cows, "Unto Yama I give thee."

Yama pleased by this offer began addressing Nachiketha, "Look Nachiketha, I am happy from your father's obligations, I am happy he has offered you, his anxiety has relieved, he is more pious, he has become sane, you have waited for three days here when I am out, kindly ask your three doubts straight to me." This is what the above-mentioned *Suthra* explains about.

Nachiketha had only three *Varam* (wishes) to Yama—

Anthaa Sankalpaha Sumana Yethasyad Itamaanyur
Gowthamabhi Mrithyuhu

Tva Prassanno Abhivedaath Praatha Ethath
Thrayanyam Prathama Varam Vrune.

Addressing Yama as *Gowthama,* Nachiketha airs his first wish to Yama, "My father is free from anger, anxiety, depression and delusion. Kindly accept my greetings *O* Lord Yama. I am sure you set me free. This is my first wish."

Lord Yama answers Nachiketha as—"My young child, in similar fashion earlier I have made Uddalaki son of Aruna to sleep peacefully with no anxiety (in *Mano Dharma* the anxiety is considered as death. Hence, removing a person's anxiety is like offering rebirth). I have brought back this young boy from the jaws of death *O* Nachiketha."

At this juncture, I am not going to explain all; now, Nachiketha asked for a second *Varam* (wish). Nachiketha is known for his innocence. He asks Yama, "OYama, tell me how all who are in heaven are immortal, why not here. In heaven, do you think all are immortal because there is no 'old' there, all are peaceful, no anxiety with them, are you sure they never feel thirst, they never experience sorrow, never rejoice in enjoyments as we do in this world? Tell me faithfully, describe me honestly about this immortal business, this is my second wish O Lord."

Dear friends, this truth riddled comment is an essential arm of renouncement one can have if he possesses dignity, virtues and values. On this, Lord Yama was stunned by such a truth-oriented wish of young Nachiketha. With all sincerity and humbleness, Yama answers—

"O Nachiketha, I loved your wish, listen carefully, immaturity is a hurdle to follow dear. The fire is an endorser for this boundless world, fire is also the connector for the whole universe; fire is also the force abiding the countless secret places hidden in the heart, fire is the beginning of life, fire is the reason behind the brick at a kiln used in the construction of mind and matter, fire is energy, which takes away the fear when offered, O Nachiketha, I shall pass also the boon I possess of the fire onto you, this fire holds the foundation through a chain, listen O Nachiketha, the obeisance of fire breaks your silence on birth, life and death. And also on *Brahman* and the omniscient; knowing is only the means to bring peace, living in peace is the eternity, knowing the fire is the second wish of you for the road to heaven, the honey of fire is the essence of eternity in you. O Nachiketha, ask your third wish."

Nachiketha was pleased with the answer, "O Lord Yama, I have a third doubt, the departed do not depart totally, a part of the departed is left, the limited knowledge of mine explains, throw a light on this O Lord Yama"

Lord Yama was thrilled and astonished on this doubt of Nachiketha. He failed to give a subtle answer and he pleaded Nachiketha to ask another boon and release him from this doubt but Nachiketha insisted on Yama to answer. The explanation Lord Yama narrated on this subtle part of an individual's soul to universal souls is not that easy and it is difficult to make knowable to believe. Lord Yama tried to offer all his possessions to Nachiketha to prevent him from persisting on his wish for an answer. Young Nachiketha could have accepted all His wealth and material and he would have lived comfortably. But, for Nachiketha, it was not physical ownership, it was knowledge that he wanted from Lord Yama.

Lord Yama explains, "O Nachiketha, good you have interest on this difficult doubt, the doubt you have is actually on the conditioned soul, the imperfect soul; the perfect soul, O Nachiketha is eternal or heaven just explained, it is the sweet part of the corn, which we devour, the seed (*Pathanjali's Yoga* of seed) remains; the seed left is for our future generation, the self has the transient soul so also the permanent soul, the absolute self the *Brahman* is a universal soul that has no value with no individual soul. O Nachiketha, listen carefully, each soul quests for the eternal or the heaven abode, soul is always moulded with layers of imperfections, which it has to shed from one generation to another generation to be infinite; for soul to be immortal, it is the possession of good and to remain peaceful, the birth and the rebirth takes shape in this ever generational formula, no formula, no universe O Nachiketha."

Nachiketha was satisfied from the three wishes that was offered by Lord Yama. Nachiketha was in euphoria when he had found escaping from the jaws of death. Nachiketha was exuberant for knowing the mystery behind the *Brahman*. The reasons behind the immortality was known by him, he never possessed any doubts thereafter in his mind. Lord Buddha said, "one's anxiety, one's delusion, one's hate are characters or traits of a person living materially not morally, a rebirth is possible when all these three are shed instantaneously to be moral and human." Knowing knowledge beyond death could be a stepping-stone towards immortality. In other words, if we are not renouncing, then we are fit to be called as "*Koopa Mandukas* (frog in a well)."

The young Nachiketha would have reached a state of immortality after realising what Lord Yama wanted him to know. Could Nachiketha become immortal by discarding and disowning his ignorance? Yes, this is possible from the knowledge he would have acquired from Lord Yama. The same analogy holds good for a drug addict too. A drug addict could also postpone his end from the clutches of his death by meditating on narcotic drugs he uses and health hazards it would lead to. A person on his early recognition and diagnosis of cancer could escape from its hell by timely medical intervention. Many examples of victory over death have been explained. There are no known literatures written to escape from death. That is the beauty of death. Swamy Vivekananda conquered death in his tender age by quenching his thirst by drinking literature; he rectified his falsehood by understanding philosophy and he was happy by dispersing his possessed knowledge to the millions of people. His only effort was to leave something on earth, he won in that and accepted the much awaited death at his early age. The same or postponement of death is a near possibility if we do what Swamy Vivekananda did. Frankly, all social ills are symbolic of death. People are walking, eating and working but they are dead to themselves by possessing horrific sensuous thoughts. Parents are dead to their wards who are actually drug addicts, psychopaths, deviants and with borderline personalities. Paradox to this statement is that the death of these wards is the will of their parents. A glimpse of Swami Vivekananda's mind is possible with knowledge but not with the corrupt practice or ill preaching people. *Athman* is neither pure nor impure but through our pure thinking and by our good deeds we leave a message printed on *Athman* to pass on to the next generation. It is like a silicon chip in our computers, but the same type of chip within us is our carbon chip or genes. That is why I call death as a merchant, he can purchase death by our illness that affects mind or body but the same death can be sold or postponed if we are able to know the knowledge and also when we practice dispersing the known knowledge to others. Innocence and compassion are two strong points for the mind to attain wisdom. Hence, the role of *Vidhi* is for those who are studded with impurity. In the mean thinkers, possessing immoral feelings, following ethos-less attitude, and violence-oriented individuals, the *Vidhi* is a nice cliché. This is my second *Aramis* or second *Musketeer* of death.

She was young, only seven years old, when while taking a walk with her father, she found a few people gathered in front of one of the houses where a pyre was lit on the road pavement, with smoke billowing. She could hear sobs and she also could see mourning of the members of this deceased family. It is easy to diagnose that there was death of one of the family members. She asked a question to her father, "Daddy, why is there a pyre in front of the dead person's house?" Her father could not answer. Her father actually is a friend of mine who wanted an answer for his daughter's question. It was a weird question to me, though I was not in a position to answer him immediately. Candidly, I had borrowed some time to answer him. When I was alone, I tried to find a connection between pyre ritual with the natural or the unnatural death in a Hindu family. I found an answer for her innocent question, which may not be accepted by many; still I would wish to explain. The person who is deceased is already dead, but for the family members he is not dead. Hence, the pyre they lit is more of a symbolic ritualistic procedure that the life of the deceased still persists inside his body. Dead bodies are always cold, which the deceased relatives and friends would not accept so easily. Pyre exist until the relatives and friends have a last glimpse of this dead man. After confirmation and acceptance by kith and kin, the dead will have a last journey to the graveyard, and then this pyre is officially dosed off. Understand the paradox; man's life source is smoke rather than fire. Fire is a source for this universal origin. We all, including the matter, are thrown out particles from the mega *Spoota* (great explosion), which is said to have taken place approximately fifty million years ago at some point in this *Brahman.* Fire cannot be fire always because it engulfs whole life and also the matter. Smoke is the driving component of man's awareness. If smoke turns to fire, then our bodies get roasted. Hence, this smoke keeps life moving till one's death arrives and even after his death for a few hours. In this time, it is for the relatives to arrive and have a last glimpse (*Darshan*) of the deceased. This ritual is important to near ones of the deceased because denial could lead to frank grief. Hence, acceptance of such a loss relieves depression. If this ritual does not exist or is not performed duly, then there could be extended grief or frank psychiatric disorders. Hence, this girl is third Muskeeter, Prothos to me.

If we travel deep into the questions posed by these three young girls, all have one common connotation, which is innocence behind their questions on death. This is exactly the reason why I call these three youngsters who posed the questions as three musketeers of death. Are they not con-brio?

KUMBH (The Mind Full)

In our Hindu culture, for all auspicious ceremonial occasions, at the onset, we perform a ritual of carrying *Kumbh Kalasa* (pots filled with sacred water) by girls who have not attained menarche. Why only girls? Why not those in their sweet sixteen's? In *Upanishath,* a girl is always thought to be pure but not a girl who had already attained menarche. Truly speaking, my theory is not because she had attained menarche, this is because of the sex hormones released out of their biological clock that is said to have induced impurities in their minds. God has never asked a menstruating woman not to come inside a temple. He avoids menstruating girls or women because of their irritability, inattention the hormones could produce and lack of concentration they suffer during their menstrual period. It is said or thought that her clarity of thinking too would come down in this period. Hence, whatever she wants to offer in her prayers to God would be partial, not total. In psychiatry, the same condition has been termed as Pre-menstrual tension, which is curable with mere counselling and also by the prescription of mild antidepressants. Many things have been narrated in the literature about the said natural biological process of a woman. According to me, the narration I narrated could be a probable reason why God does not allow such woman inside the Sanctum sanctorum during menstrual period. Today, menstrual fluid is a life source for stem cells, which are separated and reused in certain emergency surgical conditions or neurological conditions for the respective tissues to regenerate. When such is the value of this menstrual fluid, then what made us to think a woman as inferior?

Kumbh Kalasa (metallic pottery filled with water), which they carry, is filled with water up to the brim of the container. Pundits collect water from the flowing river if present adjacent to ritual places or from any source to their advantage. The water they collect basically represents *Matha Ganga* (mother Ganga). Such a *Kumbh* is placed on a place of importance and with *Vedic Manthras* (sacred chanting) invoke Goddess *Ganga Matha* with all fervour, sanctity and piety. One should know that this *Kumbh* is not half-filled but completely filled. There is a well know proverb in Kannada, "*Thumbida Koda Thulakalla* (half-filled pot creates noise, completely filled pots do not produce noise)" What does this statement mean? The answer is *Mouna* or silence, because half-filled potteries always produce noise. On one exact day, once in twelve years, for all planetary degrees and altitudes in which planets travel or move, there will be an earth tilt from south to north, the sun that was far away from life moves more near to the life from this tilt of the earth. The cold side of the life withers and the warm side of life reappears; this time of the day, is called *Mouna Amavasya.* The same event perennially is been called *Makara Sankranthi* (beginning of the harvest season) festival, which is been performed with much hype every year in a few states of our country. On this day, in *Kumbh Mela* (conglomeration), in the *Sangam* (merging point) of rivers near *Prayag* (sacred place in North India), people, *Sanths, Gurus and Nagas* in millions take the holy dip. In our life, what would *Mouna* convey? My *Guru Mouna Muni* always asserts, "Silence is the only one who is a true friend, silence is the only one who is everything and silence is the only way for us to transcend." This is exactly what Pathanjali called in his *Suthra* as *"Evam Shunyam"* or 'as if vacuum.' Mahatma Gandhi conveyed this method of meditative practice as *Mouna* to the whole world as an instrument of renunciation and a means for compassion. The noise in the brain is otherwise called as the confusion of mind. In psychiatry, this *Mouna* has a role to play under unconventional management of psychiatric neurotic disorders. This treatment can also be called as the *Mouna* Therapy, just like the music therapy. There are different types of meditative techniques, which have been performed by many *Sages* as an austerity (*Thapas*) measure. Many *Rishi Munis* performed austerity for many years to appease their respective Gods to get more and more personal powers. This has been well documented in our mythological scriptures. Some *Rishi Munis* used sanctioned powers after appeasing many Gods for good purposes and others used the same for bad purposes.

Kumbh is basically a small metal pottery made of pure copper for the upper class and steel for the lower class, which holds any form of liquid placed in an upright position. Hence, a liquid or water in such positions is always seen as full when pottery is filled to its capacity. If this position is altered or inverted, the pot liquid spills all over. In Vedanthic analysis, our head is as a pottery placed in an inverted fashion, which is not able to hold any liquid. Hence, always our scriptures convey that our brain is half–filled, at least symbolically. Because of this de facto position, our head is always noisy. The explanation narrated by me is purely my hypothesis. *Kumbh* has only one opening, whereas our head has seven openings. They are two nostrils, two eyes, two ears and one mouth. One would expect that our mind disturbances are because of the functional incongruity from such different openings. If ears are closed, other openings refuse to comply. In this dichotomy, our incoming signals would not be processed effectively at any given point of time. So, invariably, an individual's clear thinking eludes. Hence, this type of thinking leads to confusion. Confusion in the mind leads to anxiety; this anxiety creates despondency, finally depression, with antecedents as abnormal behaviours.

Today we have wonderful molecules of antidepressants but in our earlier days to overcome this disturbed mental state these molecules were a distant dream to the disturbed persons. Hence, meditation, *Thapas* (austerity) and different rituals were many paths for the management of human fear, anxiety and depression. *Mouna* was one of the many meditative techniques followed from time immemorial. Hence, in *Kumbh,* a seeker tries to seek the *Urja* or *Ananda* (bliss) in the *Sangama* (meeting point of rivers), where conglomeration of these rivers would create mystique tunes of the divine music, which can be experienced and heard only in a state of our utter silence. This is done especially in *Mouny Amavasya* (no moon day), where in this silence or in this state of meditation, the person is said to attain the maximum bliss because the calming tiny moon could also be a detractor for our total silence. Therefore, "The music, the meditation and the mathematics of the mind thus obtained are of the highest value and near virtuous."

On this said day, by performing *Mouna*, we are trying to mix our mind with three different planes of *Vedhanthic* world. They are the *Sthoola* or the body, the *Suukshma* or the psyche and the *Karana* or the knowing. Same trilogy holds good for Oneness between the body, the mind and the soul. The same explanation could also be given to Alfred Sigmund's identity, ego and superego. It is not a simple task to adopt such high form of adeptness. This could be obtained by a seeker when there is a *Shrama* or the energy, *Shraddha* or the patience and *Bhava* or the total involvement. It is said that to achieve this face is a herculean task and the austerity cannot be completed in one year but actually this meditative accomplishment would require twelve long years. And it is also said that such powers one could see or possess with *Nagas* (one of the religious Hindu groups) settled in the banks of Ganges. This is exactly the reason why on *Mouny Amavasya* (no moon day with extreme silence) the members of *Naga Akadas* are allowed to have first *Shahi* (sacred) or *Snan* (dip) in the river *Sangam* (near a place called Buddha Prayag in north India). *Naga* is said to perform strong *Brhama Charya* (celibacy) and other difficult rituals to become a true *Yogi*. They are ready for all these twelve years to accept the *Deeksha* (obtain powers) from their respective *Guru's* on the day of *Mouna Amavasya*.

Lakhs and lakhs of devotees visit *Kumbh Mela* to have a holy dip to get rid of their sins they have committed for all their twelve years of existence to attain immediate *Moksha* or liberation. This liberation (*Moksha*) is symbolically meant for those who after taking a holy dip should not be reborn again. Thinking in this line, I find more of their ignorance; it is foolish to think that we all stop here forever in this life progression after taking a dip at the *Sangam*. We do come back once again through our genes inherited, which will be passed on to our progenies. To explain in simple terms, I have an attitude, behaviour and creativity, which I transmit to my son or daughter while I am living. Therefore, these constructs are mine even after my death. This is how I assert

Vedanthically that I would come back in my next generation too. In Science, I call this as gene transmission to my offspring and their ultimate expression later as Reincarnation. This is an ever-continuing saga of this Universe. This is exactly the reason why I call *Athman* (soul) as all-pervading and eternal. By such possessed refined gene, possessor should always abide to the Natural Law and should not be an abettor to the ills of Statutory Law. Given a chance, I want to be there in the *Kumbh Mela.* For me, one minute of silence every day is sufficient to attain little *Moksha.* In this silence, I refine my past sins and such refined information would have found a slot in my genes so that this gene would travel to my next generation for a better offspring. This phenomenon I also call as *Karma* Philosophy. Therefore, I may not come back with the same name or form in my next generation, but I do come back with good thinking and actions through my progeny, who has a name and form. Many great *Sages* and famous people are remembered for their writings and actions. Mere acceptance by people of our society leaves a *Mouny* of credited austerity (literary people or altruistic people) to be called as a complete man or as an eternal *Purush.*

CRIMINAL INDEX
(An Index Much Needed)

After it rains in the evening, the next morning, I always take a walk. Walking would bring the necessary nectar and the ambrosia to my mind due to the pleasant atmosphere of the post-rain environment. While walking, I came across a wayside parked lorry on the road; the owner of this lorry was yelling at the cleaner, who was asleep inside the cabin after a hard day's work. It was eight in the morning; it was habitual for the owner to shout at the cleaner. I was touched by the cleaner's shabby dress, unkempt face and clumsy movements. Mere observation of this scene by any ordinary person with his inadequate knowledge would guess that the cleaner hailed from a poor socio-economic strata and he had migrated from a nearby village or from a distant state. Presently, in any given city, such migratory youths are increasing in their numbers day by day, with an intention of trying their luck to seek suitable jobs or to try their hands to settle down with a lucrative business. Lately, this migration has led to psycho-socio-political injustice to innumerable youths in our metros. Uneducated, ignorant, aspiring adolescents pour in thousands and thousands every year to our great cities. In these circumstances, a shabby and sham approach by the respective people's representatives allowed the growth of many social evils in the cities. I was reading an article wherein a sports minister of that country, which was ready to host World Cup of football, had asked to the police to accompany the football players from their respective countries to safeguard their own players and also to protect their own accompanying tourists. Today, such is the magnitude of psycho-social criminal chaotic atmosphere we face in our large cities. This anarchy has gone beyond the control of any government. If the government is ready to reach the confused and anxious youth by giving them proper education, job opportunity and minimum safety near to their geographical places, probably the exodus or mass migration would have been prevented and in turn the criminal index could have scaled down.

Frankly, it is our enormous population growth with antecedent problems that are the main cause for increase in the criminal index, but the wisdom and the farsightedness of the government could prevent such heinous crimes, though not completely. Today's technologies have an access to such people for their cheap entertainment. One of many such technologies is the mobile phone. Today, these mobile phones are loaded with pornography and dirty MMSs. I do agree that such acts or continuous watching of porno by the young would cause boredom, but the obsessions and the drugs used by the young would certainly increase the risk of crime against the innocent. Crime does not take place after watching such things immediately but takes place when there is an opportunity or after some prompt from the environment. This could be one of the many reasons why we are noticing an increase in the percentage of rapes and murders today. As density of such groups increase, so also the slums keep increasing in our cities. For a sociologist, it is easy to say that in such an atmosphere, the crime rate also increases. I am not a sociologist, but being a psychiatrist, I have a different view on this. I think in terms of prevention of crimes rather than treating and managing such criminals. Basic problems of criminology and also the causes of such crimes have been discussed all over the world under different titles, such as one's economy, the typical family, familial predisposition, many social issues, individual education, their peer relationships, environmental reasons and so on and so forth. For me, the matter to be considered is if our society with its morality apt to call them as criminals. Actually, we do not have any moral grounds to call them as abnormal because we as normal have not provided much to what they are really entitled to. For example,

- ✓ We have not provided free education to them.
- ✓ We are unable to provide professional help to them.
- ✓ We are far behind to engage good teachers to teach them.
- ✓ Our education system is expensive for their good education.
- ✓ We provide no minimum infrastructures for them to embark on seeking good jobs.
- ✓ We have no way to provide potable water (arsenic and other toxic materials in drinking water have been shown to increase the criminal index due to their toxic effects on CNS) to them.
- ✓ We are yet to implement right to education for the deprived.
- ✓ We have confusion regarding implementing sex education as a curriculum in our schools.
- ✓ We have made no effort to reduce poverty.
- ✓ We have brought education into the folds of many religions.

- ✓ There are different castes and innumerable creeds, which are the deterring factors for our progress.
- ✓ Bringing reservation in higher education would not be an act of humanity, as politicians think.
- ✓ There is a lack of proper law enforcement to stop or to minimise the criminal index.
- ✓ There is an improper empowering provision to the respective legal institutions by the Government agency for controlling crimes.
- ✓ There is a lack of providing minimum socio-economic equality and also we have allowed the different economic statuses in the society to grow, which would have led to increase in the criminality index.
- ✓ Our politicians and bureaucrats have indulged in high level of corruption.
- ✓ There is involvement or indulging in corrupt practices at the professional level.
- ✓ We have not allowed the partial media free: media has not learnt the ethics of the society and there is a lacuna in the Governmental effort to curb easy access to bad information and technology.
- ✓ There is no agency to counter and check improper counselling techniques in our country.
- ✓ We have not created an awareness program for the public for the bad effects of listening to self-styled *Dongi* Gods and self-styled Goddesses.
- ✓ There is a lack of will to go beyond our intelligence.
- ✓ We have failed in initiating proper resilient attitude with the people.

- ✓ We have failed in patenting our cultural values and ethos like *Yoga*
- ✓ We are not portraying important ancient icons by bringing goodness in our school curriculum, etc.

If these statements of mine are correct, then what could a confused young population in our country give us in return? As a practicing psychiatrist, I would like to bring to the notice of the readers a condition called Common Single Room Bug's Syndromes. These syndromes come under homosexuality, with antecedent innumerable problems, with various drug abuses and consequent criminal outcomes. The medical fraternity of European Union is discussing on the Super Bug of India. Both are notorious to society and also for humans, respectively, for their power in destroying. Knowing and understanding both would first lower the criminality index and lessen mortality rate. Generally, if we view the role of our parents or our caretakers in such circumstances, how can they diminish the crime index? The theory is satisfactory, but is it applicable practically? For all such circumstances, we cannot always blame their parents, if there is anything to blame it is their Genes or *Karma* with their neuronal structure with antecedent expressions. Basically, criminality is a mindset, fueled and propagated on a faulty brain limbic engine. These sorts of mind sets also get accentuated from the adults around them to make their ends to fulfil. Good society and better education does help them but counselling and spirituality (good spirituality) could move dorsally placed imperfect neuronal tracts into front portion of functional brain. This would enhance the effectiveness of neo-encephalon (forebrain) functions of human.

If an EEG is recorded and studied on an epileptic patient, the classical spike and wave picture of the EEG would made the neurologist hundred percent sure of his clinical diagnosis. If there are no such inter-ictal (period between two attacks of fits) activities, it does not mean that a person with epilepsy is not an epileptic. In the similar fashion, a crime committed in episodes and when tried legally, it means he is a criminal. For criminals not having such records, we cannot rule out that they do not have the criminal mask. So, criminality is an opportunistic and cue oriented activity and also the act of criminality is more impulsive in nature and a compulsive phenomenon. Pre-meditated crimes do not come under this clause, because basically they are materialistic oriented. Practically, sketch-mediated acts cannot be an impulsive act, hence pre-meditation in a crime always carries a high degree of punishment. Any impulsive acts with barbaric, heinous and brutal killings should be considered as rarest of rare, and irrespective of age, the legal institution should put them in the gallows. Today, all over our country, the intelligentsia, Government, legal institutions and Non-Governmental Organisation (NGO)s are discussing about the legalisation of prostitution. My thinking on this would be that by legalising prostitution, would it bring down rapes and crimes on women? My simple answer is, No. Why? One should be thoughtful enough to understand this statement, which I am going to narrate here.

An act which is pleasure oriented is only to relieve or to discharge the urge. This act of an individual under legal terms does not come under the severe punishment group. Recently, the same act is been included under IPC section, under which the said act is non-bailable offence. My point of contention is that whether these frequent changes or amending the laws would bring the crime rate down? According to me, time is the only factor that could throw a glimpse of light on this question. After the assault on a girl or on a woman, the anxiety created or fear of getting identified creeps in the persons mind. Then he hatches an idea, immediately or slowly, to kill and dispose off the person related to the crime. Such kind of criminal timid acts drive them to kill the innocents. This extreme violence they adopt only to avoid facing heavy punishment later. This is why after acting viciously their mind forces them to do such heinous acts of killing. Absence of morality and defiant attitude are also the other causes. These acts are most punishable under the law if these criminal acts are proved beyond any doubt by providing proper document and witnesses by the investigating agency. It is unfortunate to know that these acts or crimes do happen under the influence of narcotic drugs they consume. For any normal thinking man, a question would arise, "What is the role of parents in curbing such acts? Can parents have any mechanism to watch these wards for all the twenty-four hours?" In my practice, I have come across many dyslexics for counselling. The basic problem with many such students is that they do not understand the subjects like science and mathematics because of which they find an easier way of leading their life. This type of relaxed way of getting gratification comes due to their lack of knowledge. Reading and studying always requires more energy and hard work. In cases of learning disorders, student's lack both; thus, they find the easiest way by reaching out to bad elements in the society. They become a prey and are trapped, from where they cannot escape. When they try to escape, they are chased and others inflict injuries on them. In these conditions, the role of parents, police, professional mental health personnel, legal system, government agencies and NGOs play some role rather than the complete role. From my experience, any form of aggressive medical or non-medical managements of these cases simply fails. Hence, to my knowledge, a small group of these children with dyslexia who have criminal intentions improved satisfactorily.

Coming to the point of this Bug Syndrome, the possible way of managing is by instituting a governmental social reform institute or quarantine centers at all the city peripherals. These institutes should be run effectively by the government by appointing professional mental health people, sociologists, reformers and spiritual counsellors. For these institutes, there will be a heavy burden to the exchequer of the state. This could be a possibility for the head of the state who has good vision and who is determined to tackle corruption and crime at grassroot levels. This approach probably might bring down the crime rate. If crime is a disease, it has to be treated as any psychiatric disorder in mental hospitals.

Why did I take the cleaner as an example? If enforcers put such people into a proper night stay dormitories, I think criminal index drastically would come down. In the era of information technology, personal identification codes could also help in reducing the crime rates. Therefore, these are the only ways to reach the confused young in our society. Good scientific approach and future further studies, proper statistical analysis, technologically integrating crime with information, better funds by the government, etc. are all welcome to minimise criminality or to convert our country into crime-free state.

WALKING DEAD (Man's True Nature)

I watch occasionally good movies; one such movie was Walking Dead. I was impressed a lot with this movie, as one emotional nun moved heaven and earth to prevent the death penalty to a rape and murder convict who had committed the act of murder on a young couple enjoying their honeymoon in the deep wood. At the end of the movie, this struggling nun had left no stone unturned in her effort to save this convict from the lethal injection. She expresses her deep sorrow to the family of this dead convict, as she could not save this convict. She was unable to conceal her sadness for not providing ultimate life, which was entitled to him by the grace of God. She felt that this convict would have continued the God-given life if federal law would not punish him with the lethal injection. This movie had only an emotional content but today such trial of condemnation has a political obnoxious odour. This odour is so repelling and nauseating that after mixing this odour with political clout, the mixed aroma thus produced has turned into pungent smell. Sniffing this pungent smell drives people crazy because it has penetrated so deep into our apparel, which everybody has to bear forcibly. We are all intelligent blinds, with no suitable answers for these politico-socio-psychopathic events. Our freedom in our land have been caned, arrested and locked inside the golden cages. Hence, we are all happy with the gold but not with our freedom. My personal view is that hanging as punishment for heinous crimes is not at all an answer. If these acts are unless otherwise proved beyond doubt at any given point of time and place, till then they are innocent. This is true to the thinking of many enlightened masters. Clipping ones wings is more than sufficient to make him 'walk dead.' But, the propensity of crime like pre-meditation, barbaric nature of these acts, and heinous part of the act committed and the perverted approach to the killing definitely calls for a rethinking on charging or punishing such convicts with death penalty.

This is one side of the story. Frankly, we all walk physically, but psychologically, we are the walking dead. There are reasons to say so, and they are:

- ✓ Political appeasements.
- ✓ Subversion by money and muzzle.
- ✓ Talking double standards.
- ✓ Pervading corruptive practices.
- ✓ Hierarchical practices.
- ✓ Imposing restrictions to our freedom.
- ✓ Disintegrating value systems.
- ✓ Bad effects of virtual information technology, etc.

All these have made man dead in all aspects. Systematic snubbing and silencing the social voices against governmental evils answers all. At a fast-paced progress in our econometric materialism, men are increasingly being devoid of emotions; meanwhile, attachments to the innumerable worldly glitters are increasing. Men are falling prey for naïve paranoiac world and the gap between human bondages is widening. Hence, fear and confusion is present all over the world with added despondency and depression, which are doubling. The values behind plurality are fast disappearing; meanwhile, singularities are increasing. Still, all is not that bad because knowledge has found a quantum jump but humanistic understanding finds no quantum jump. Finding societal views is only the addition and not the subtraction, or in other words, to be optimistic one has to believe in arithmetical multiplication rather than in algebraic multiplication. If all of us remove subtraction and division in our value system, probably our next generation has definite answers for human's negative feelings. If we are able to:

- ✓ Bring mutual trust.
- ✓ Involve in-group participation.
- ✓ Find the methods of meditation.
- ✓ Find a way for improving methods or inventing psycho-societal instruments for better understanding.
- ✓ Refining our expressive techniques.
- ✓ Find a means to handle many ills, etc.

All these can bring back the glory, which we have lost. By this way we all could transform ourselves into *Manus* (knowledgeable Sages) of *Manvantara* (an era when sages outnumbered ordinary people) period. This requires whole-hearted participation by the society and as well as from the Government agencies. When this attitude is achieved by a man, then naturally he is walking as a man but not as a dead man. In the epic Mahabaratha, Arjuna (one of the prince of the *Kuru* dynasty) was called *Maha Bahoo* (mighty shoulders), meaning the possessor of two great shoulders that saw no defeat. In the similar fashion, two *Bahoo* (shoulders) are there in our life, they are the smiles and the trust, which could make a big difference in this dying society.

Many convicts in the prison might have been innocents who are waiting for their verdict. Without hundred percent evidence by the enforcing agency, hanging an ignorant convict would lead to murder. If this statement of mine is true, then who punishes this said agency after awarding such a sentence? The only instrument, which can avoid all such ugly natures of the government, law and police system, is the *Sakshi Bhava* or the 'self-witness.' This is exactly what Ashtavakra (saint with eight deformities) preached to us that 'we are the witness to the relative reality of our *Chitha* (mind).' Hence, we are all Doers (seekers). I was fascinated by *Naksha Agocharaha* (scene not seen) phrase from Ashtavakra, which says that our eyes are tuned for the worldly vision, not tuned for the wisdom of vision. If we are able to tune ourselves to the vision of wisdom then the *Gochara* (seen) by us would change ourselves to, "I am not the doer (seeker would be the God or the man above all)" state.

AURA (The SWAMIJIS Possess)

Body is made up of condensed particles and has its own complex electromagnetic radiations, which are otherwise called as Aura. There was a patient in his seventies who came to me along with his wife to treat depression along with anxiety. He was a voracious reader of spiritual books and considered himself as a reincarnation of Lord Buddha. His wife had reported that some time back her husband would wake up in the middle of the night and attain a posture or he would sit like Buddha on the bed. She had also reported that on a few occasions, he would sit naked and also he would pressurise his wife to follow him as he would have possessed some extra powers in his mind. He had retired from his tenure as lecturer from a north eastern state. He had four children, but one son had died of some disease, another son left home, the daughter who completed her degree education was an addict to various substances of addiction and divorced twice with two children now living with a person belonging to a different religion. Another son was serving in the army and would call his father as a Bastard. Look at the quantum of problems he had in his family. He was a hypertensive and not a diabetic. Any thought of his children would drive his BP to two hundred systolic. Thankfully, he never experienced an acute cerebro vascular accident (CVA). His wife was an orthodox, living quietly with all the sufferings. This person was the kind who do not listen to anyone and would appear little inadequate in his approach to life. Whom do we blame? Is his *Aura* to be blamed?, Is his biological genetic inherent system to be blamed?, Is his upbringing at fault?, Is the freedom he permitted to his children be blamed?, Is his working place, where drugs and related problems are rampant, to be blamed?, Does the problem lie with his children?, etc.

As I was also an avid reader of *Vedic* or Spiritual books, out of interest I had asked him a question, "What do you mean by spiritualism?" He had answered as usual in his broken language, which I could not understand, but I am sure his answer was not a formal thought disorder. He had bought a book, which has narrations about the *Kundalini* (neuronal plexus). After reading this book, he would have learnt an art of stimulating his *Kundalinis* on his own, and by doing so, he would have thought that by practicing the art of *Kundalini* stimulation he would attain *Moksha* (liberation). When I had asked to bring this book to read, he had brought it promptly to my clinic and I glanced through the book. This book was written by some swamiji, whose name I do not remember. When I read this book, I found that it was not even an elementary level of Vedanthic teachings. It does not mean that I am a master of *Kundalini* or Enlightened Master. In this book, what was mentioned as *Aura* was repeated thirty or forty times in one page. This book comprised of eighty-five pages, excluding the preface. This was how my curiosity increased on *Aura* (radiance).

I searched many books to find this strange phenomenon. After knowing a little about this, I felt amazed to see Lord Buddha, who had an aura which was restricted to his head only, whereas Lord Christ had an aura to his whole body. This difference between these great Gods really confused me. If physics is right, then the aura of Lord Christ is understandable but not Lord Buddha's. According to the atomic quantum physics, any particle was derived out of some reaction inferred through *Guna* (state) and *Lakshana* or by simple properties of this derived particle. For example, energy of this particle with its specific wavelengths and its motion in the time and space would determine the name of this particular atomic particle. This is exactly what scientists are searching for in the elusive particle in the great Large Hadron Colliders (LHC) at CERN laboratory, God's particle or Higgs Boson particle. Therefore, for all practical purposes, any existing material particle has to change or has to move so as to say that it is a matter, even if it is in a stagnant position to an onlooker. Examples are the possessed gold and diamonds.

Many people have gold and diamonds stocked in their lockers, but these elements are not keeping silence. To become gold and diamond there will be a process of unfelt and unknown high resolution and energy emission taking place between millions and trillions of atoms, which are holding the gold and diamond firmly. It is basically a magnetic property. If this property is changed by applying energy, like heat or cold, these basic elements lose their original property and become diamond-less or gold-less forms. This is otherwise called as Kelvin Bose property. At 365 degrees temperature, no life or matter exists on earth, as their all-moving property gets stagnated. Hence, gold and diamond that exists in this world is relative rather than absolute.

Coming back to this aura or radiance, religious heads also do work with this magnetism principle, not similar the physicists. The Lord Buddha's aura was limited to his head. What could be the possible reason for this? Why aura did not eject out from his body? Let me explain this phenomenon, which might not be true, just an attempt from my side. It is clear that aura is secondary to matter. The head of Lord Buddha is made up of organic mass and so also his body, then why only his head emits an aura? To understand this mystical phenomenon one should be meditative. What is neutron star? For a layman, it is a dying star, highly charged nucleus at the center with enormous gravitational force emitting high energy into the universe with shockwaves all over in space. The energy produced pushes proton in its way producing Cosmic energy from the friction in its journey from far deep. In case of Lord Buddha, the exact opposite had happened because the *Chitta* (mind) which is a micro cosmos by way of enlightenment has no known nucleus in his organic brain and thus lacks gravitational pull but his brain was emitting high-powerful energy outside in the form of light called as "Compassion." Because of this reason or treachery, Buddha was asked to leave our country. Those who had strong gravitational or magnetic nucleus in their heads settled well in our country. Buddha knew that the art of meditation was silence only; hence, his aura was emitted to a few neighbouring countries. In this silence, the countries that accepted him are striving high but in our country we are starving while the fake Swamys are thriving. It is unfortunate to know that in our country only few downtrodden sectors of our people have accepted his aura. For me the limited aura of Lord Buddha is gold and diamond. It is his total *Nirvana* or *Moksha* or transcendence of individual micro cosmos or enlightened cosmic energy of pure understanding and reasoning that allowed young Siddhartha to become a man of knowledge in the prelude to become Buddha, the knower. Hence, the Master of knowing would not possess the gravitational or magnetic aura, he has only accepting aura. With this aura, he is as light as cotton, he would emit compassion, he would forgive us, and he would not attract gold or diamond. In Christianity, the very symbols of religion, which have the affinity for Lord Christ, by default are the true compassionate people, as we see with sisters in the Christian hospitals and nuns in the Christian schools.

WIFE AND WI-FI (Prelude to Separation)

I keep reading *Vedic* books. Reading cajoles me, mesmerises me and in the meantime gives food for my thoughts. After reading *Shiva Purana* a little, what I found was that for our eternal bondage, the role of Goddess Parvathi to Lord Shiva was unexplainable. There is a good old thought that for every man's success or for his achievements his other half (his wife) would be a driving force. Look at this paradox, as per the said statement, if a man wants to shine, is it the temperament (the face or the mind?) of his wife a sole responsibility? I humbly ask the reader not to take the previously mentioned sentence literally. A man who had built his company on his own, he had made his company known worldwide and also he had introduced India to the American people as Bengaluru had said when somebody had asked him about his achievement, "For my present success and extraordinary achievement, my wife's soul is the sole responsibility." This was the story behind such men's achievements but it is not true with some politicians. Politicians out of their busy schedule invariably forget their spouses. It is their problem but for me this Lord Shiva and Goddess Parvathi relationship has lot to convey to the people. Read this, I may not be correct.

Goddess Parvathi, who is sitting on Lord Shiva's lap, keeps on talking too much, but the all-knowing Lord Shiva only smiles with occasional nods and he would have never uttered a single word to her. According to *Shiva Purana,* Shiva is the life provider and also the destroyer. We are all lucky because until now he has not destroyed us and as well as this wonderful world. The reason behind the life protection or the life destruction is Goddess Parvathi as the sole reason. Lord Shiva has enormous power under his armoury but he is still (unmoving) or silent, with only smiles and with frequent nods. His destructing power is directly proportional to the words he utters; hence, He has to keep Himself snug for all of life to move in this world. The compassionate wife of his is always siting near to him watching his pulse every second to absorb all the energy, if at all he emits energy verbally. That is how the concept of *Linga* and *Youni* in Veda or Purana is in vogue today. By this story, it is probably understandable that our life exists because of Goddess Parvathi. Hence, for the success of our life and the existence of matter, Lord Shiva's wife Parvathi was the truly responsible. With this statement, it is definite that Goddess Parvathi was the conceiver and Lord Shiva was the energy provider.

This is fine in the Purana (ancient scripts). But, what actually happens in our real life? The above said depiction symbolically is meant for *Pavithra Bandhana* (sacred attachment). The concept of *Mangala Suthra* (sacred thread) is for the *Pavithratha* (virtue) and for the *Bandhana* (alchemy). The "*Mangala*" noun is otherwise represented as *Shubha Dayaka* (happy future). The *Suthras* (dossiers) always have hidden meanings like software of an operating system in computers. This had been dealt well by Pathanjali *Maha Rushi* in his one hundred ninety-three dossiers. After *Vedic* marriage, the life should be like a rosary bead or *Mallige*

Hara (jasmine bead). Hence, initially bride being a *Bhavana Swaroopi* (iconic feelings) accepts only *Mallige Huvu* (jasmine flowers). As men, I hardly find it fit to offer *Mallige Huvu* to one's wife. Because, men are mainly charged with dopamenergic drive instead of oxytocin. This is exactly what happens in many of our marriages. If this is the true perspective of a marriage, then there could be possibility of many problems creeping in their marriages. What would happen? Wife sits on husbands lap like Parvathi who sits on Shiva's lap. Husbands and wives' adamant postures would lead to *Galata* (noise), where in the case of Goddess Parvathi who does make noise, but still persists with acceptance. Goddess Parvathi in this acceptance is ready to receive energy, whereas, many wives are not ready to receive or accept any sort of energy whatsoever. Therefore, there is a discharge, a waste discharge. Because of this, many divorces are occurring. This is otherwise called "*Thu thu main main*", a political neologism. Hence, for a man to be successful, the woman behind such success should possess qualities of absorbing dopaminergic energy. If it goes waste, then she cannot be a woman responsible for his success. This should not be from one side, it has to be from either side, then only the marriages would be *Rasa Maya* (sweet or good alchemy). This is the reason why we worship *Ardha Nariswara*, half man and a half woman God. I am explaining all my narrations in an extended format because there should not be anathema.

When I have a chance to travel long distances to attend conferences, I watch many airports where men and women are with their other half in the form of laptops on their laps. This is because of the locally available free Wi-Fi (depends on availability of free Wi-Fi) connections. For me Wi-Fi is weird and fictitious and also it is a creaky, sleek, handy idiot box but for IT professionals and business people, this laptop is a Pandora Box. For a macho, an obsessive dopemaniac man, laptop would be a source of Viagara too. This box being a technological spouse does discharge energy, which has deleterious effects on the women and also on the men. According to some studies, this energy has deleterious effect on the production of testosterone and oestrogen. Because of this energy loss, it results in divorce in such couples. In this neo-technological world, for a man to be successful in his achievements, it is not the wife who is behind his success but it is his technological half, his Laptop. In this trilogy, a common factor is 'discharge.' In the first case, the discharge discussed is being compassion, the second discharge is meant for lust and the third discharge is the discharge into the invented information technologies. Meditating on these three discharges one might ignite his consciousness as to understand himself in the society best and his own invented technology better, so as to lead a good life in the future.

SUSPENDED PARTICLES (To Ponder on)

My friend is an ophthalmologist with whom I spend my free time over a cup of tea. I love tea more than alcohol. My wife name is Smt Chaya, hence, friends call me as Dr *Chaya Pathi* (*Chaay* means tea in Hindi and *Pathi* word is meant for husband in Kannada). When I was having tea in his consulting chamber, a patient had come to him with a history of brightness in his eyes. After examining the patient, my friend diagnosed him with having floaters or suspended particles present in the vitreous chambers. I had forgotten whether it was anterior or posterior vitreous chamber but I remember him saying particles in the liquid vitreous medium. Here the *Kirana* or the light's rays when fall on these glassy particles, it produces various colours, which then stimulate the photos-sensitive cells on the retina and thus the patient perceives light as bright light. This concept of suspended particles of my ophthalmology friend stirred my insight to analyse its literal meaning and also beyond the literal word.

An employee for his misdeeds in a private company is immediately fired or suspended. The same would never happen in the government institutions, because a 'commission of enquiry' would have been created on an ad hoc basis only to share the looted money or vice versa. Fine, we pay income tax promptly only for them to loot maximum and to work minimum. If I divide this 'suspended' on a hypothetical divisionary technique, I found "Suspected and apprehended." Hence suspended particle is a vagabond or a drifter, so also is it with the suspended man's mind. Confusion in him drives him to anxiety and subsequent depression. Mind is a master and body is its follower. Hence, he is a worried person until he gets cleared from the enquiry commission formed. In ophthalmology, this drifting particle is in the medium of liquid 'vitreous', and in the case of man, the same drifting mind is in the medium of *Chitha* (consciousness). Hence, it is clear that 'moving' is the time and 'medium' is the space. When I raise a question as to who am I? What time and space is about? What, am I a thrown out as suspended nanoparticle? From where am I thrown out? From where am I suspended from? The answers are very much complex.

Our earth is a speck when compared to *Brahman* (universe size or universe boundary). The tiny earth actually is a suspended particle in the medium of proton and Neutron Sea. The time in which we are living is short when compared to the space around us. This could throw some knowledge on what exactly holds us and also what is that which controls this mega *Brahman*. Probably, answer to all my questions would not be possible in this present century. Cosmos means orderly, hence, the study of universe is called as Cosmology. Leaving apart earth, universe, etc., we are bothered more of sub-nanoparticles like asteroids and meteors. The *Pralayaa* (Dooms day) could be a possibility if any of these drifting sub-nano-like particles in this *Megha Brahman* hits the earth. Conjecturally life and also the *Brahman* would perish automatically. We should know that Mother Earth or the Creator is cunning enough to leave a speck of life dormant even after its total destruction. This is so if we believe in the Vedanthic reincarnation, which is a subject of great money laundering business by our present half-baked preachers, of whom we need not get scared. This is exactly what I teach to my young daughter who is scared of the future because she has not seen the good and bad part of the society and the world. All doctors should learn to alleviate the patient's anxiety first. The mental agony is more painful when compared to the physical pain because release of pain takes certain time after the injury. It is the mindset that perceives physical pain first. Hence, true pain is relative when compared to the stress we encounter. Because of this, Sage Pathanjali asks us to be utmost thorough before delivering the words and deeds to others.

Coming to the point of suspension in the universe, it is amazing to know that how a huge condensed earth is hooked into its orbit of movement and revolves around the sun in its specific axis. When we have a hypothetical vision of our solar system as a plate where sun is in the center, then actually what holds this solar system and which is the force that aligns solar system into this universe? A simple explanation for a layman would be that in the midst of the huge sea of proton and neutron, a solid condensed earth as the floater been controlled by the *Abhaya Hastha* (caring hand), which has enormous electromagnetic energy, which could have twined universe by billion and trillions of unseen powerful threads. Hence, carving Gods and Goddesses iconographies with *Abhaya Hastha* could be a probable reason behind explaining symbolically that our universe is united. Our ordinary classical vegetable *Thakkadi* (scale which could be held by hand), a small plate is suspended from a point at top with three or four strings attached to the plate edge on three or four sides respectively could throw a light on this universe or *Brahman* formation. For me these strings have an acute angle from the common point of their suspension down. If we consider the same logic for our solar system, at the top there should be a point holding the entire breadth and length of our solar system. If this is true then the source of control should be possibly from a single point one billion light years away emitting massive magnetic force on our solar system. For all our practical knowledge for such a distance, the hypothetical strings just explained are placed at ninety degree's (perpendicular). When we are sitting by the window side of an airplane thirty thousand feet above, a peak crosses our plane slowly. It is an illusion in our mind set for the distance we are in to the point of focus. This is also true with the moon, the same moon after travelling one thousand mile on road stays to its original position. What I would like to make understand is that how big our universe is or the level of magnitude of our space. Is it impossible to imagine that what universe is all about for an ordinary brain? This is what exactly the *Bhairava* means, a deity worshiped in Hindu philosophy. This *Bhairava* been portrayed as *Bibithsa* (awkward, horrifying and scary). In Vedanthic terms, this *Bhairava* is otherwise called as 'God, beyond universe.' Beyond this universe or beyond the edge of universe we do not know what lay hold of or lay hold on? Hence, he is *Bhairaveshwara* or the principle creator of such a huge *Bhairava,* otherwise called also as *Eshwara.* This is all right when space is been discussed, then what about the time? He should be called as God *Kala* (time). Hence time and space together called as *Kala Bhairava,* but in science time exists near to the mass or to the matter, hence matter is limited when compared to the space (*Jaga*). The said space is not quiescent; it has full of electromagnetic currents with innumerable strings operating on. In this sea of quanta, these strings are interconnected, inter-related, inter-dependent and inter-functional. Hence, there also matter lies and this matter is called as dark matter, which occupies around ninety-six percent of our universes. What is visible to us is only four percent. Hence, in our Hindu philosophy the other deity we worship is *Kala Bhairava,* not *Kala* alone who does not exist individually as a deity for worship. This is what actually I meant by Suspended particle. The enlightened man behind these imaginations is the real *Paraiah* or true sage where these sages could have understood these Gods. These Gods could have had futuristic multi-dimensional vision in the absence of ultra-modern laboratories housing super computers at that period. This is exactly the value and wisdom of our Hinduism at this present context. We all have name and form in time and space. The creator is magnanimous enough to give hundred years of charged battery to live on. God does not expect anything from our life. He would ask us to connect everybody with trust and smile and He would be happy if we connect ourselves with the myriads of life, the exotic flowers and esoteric fauna. This connection would become meaningful when there is a disintegration of our hard shell called Self. This could be achieved through mere understanding of what life is all about. This understanding is also a possibility after we reasoned rationally what this wonderful world is all about. Criticality has no role when it is done alone but same critique could be a passion when person finds discriminating reasons to the pinching signals, which we are getting from the outside world. Millions and trillions of signals keep hitting us daily, which are unwanted. The art of learning to take good signals and discarding dubious or bad signals is also otherwise called as *Yoga.*

SWINGERS V/S HATERS (The Pendulum)

Today's technology is progressing at a galloping pace and has found a quantum jump with consequent or antecedent innumerable health (mental and physical) hazards. If we name any technology, it has its own problem to the mankind. For example, the mobile technologies with their missed SMSs, MMSs and down loaded rape game, etc. have increased the crime rate against humankind including sexual abuses and other unwanted criminal activities. The same is also true with our television. The 24/7 news channels are like *Chat Masalas*, but some programs or channels impart lots of insight and knowledge to the viewers. Mass media is a prelude to emulate good in us from our real heroes. Today, if we enquire any working man he is so much busy in his own busy worldly schedules. Hence, all are engaged by one or another way. Inventions of mobiles today made busy people to talk in spite of their busy schedules. TRAI (Telecommunication and Regulatory Authority of India) colluding with companies have made talk in the mobile phones cheap. The time tics, pendulum swings, busy has become business and no time for the monogomic relationships. In the institution of marriage, monogamy relationships demand much time for true courtships. Such courtship would warrant an extreme *Bhavana* (feelings) and this feeling does requires a lot of learning techniques.

They never make an effort to learn so, because learning is always difficult and people feel that learning would be a waste of time. People do not want to waste huge energy unnecessarily because they want an easy way to enjoy. Hence, people are oriented towards fastness. Fastness is one type of pleasure among people. That is how candid sex emerged today. Our country is small compared to the high density of our population. Presence of Private detective agencies, invented CCTVs, mobile phones, micro, macro and hidden cameras all over made adultery a herculean task for a man to commit. There are two things a human or woman would require. One is testosterone or oestrogen and another very important hormone is oxytocin.

Presently, this is because of the following:

- ✓ People's busy schedule.
- ✓ Inadvertent access to materialistic things.
- ✓ Easy approach to commodity life in the society.
- ✓ Immediate pleasure seeking.
- ✓ Involving in dangerous games.
- ✓ Puzzles all over the world.
- ✓ Loading themselves with imaginary fear.
- ✓ Pounding self-consciousness to individual's heart.
- ✓ Increasing number of cheaters in the society.
- ✓ Upward gambling trends noticed.

Dispersion of criminal's everywhere has led to the avoidance or reduced human accessibility to bad things.

These things made people to hook for social networks, which in turn created social groups for lasting pleasures hitherto failed to enjoy by them. Such groups are called

Swingers, swinging like a pendulum from Monogomy to Orgysomy (group sex). Such things do happen under the umbrella of dangerous games. It is a taboo all over. I had a male patient who had belonged to other religion, while counselling him for his paranoid ideas "Dr, do you know orthodox Hindus enter neighbours home from the back door." When I have not observed these kinds of behaviour with any particular community, I do not bother for such statements. It is bad to talk of that which I have not seen and heard. This attitude of a professional man will have tremendous virtues in his profession. This virtue prevent bigot. This also prevents prejudice against events or happenings sojourn. I think that any sex therapist for that matter is of the opinion that testosterone and oxytocin do not present to their optimum levels at any given point of time. Both reach to its optimum levels in the blood at different times and these hormonal levels are coerced with their mind set. If by all practical purposes, both hormones present to the optimum levels at any given point of time in our blood stream then this state would be termed as true love. In ancient literature this has been dealt in detail with coded *Thanthra*. This *Thanthra* or art of *Kudalini* has been used by commercial *Swamies* under their dangerous games with antecedent money mongering and also induce problems like iatrogenic psychiatric conditions to the money spenders from their ill advices.

The *Mithuna* or sculptures at Kujaraho temple depict hard core love scenes but the cognizance and conation for such scenes are left to the observer. Worshiping deity *Rathi* and *Manmatha* has a lot of meaning in the *Kamana Habba* (Holi) a festival of colours. In this festival, burning the effigy of Kama is done with piety and fervour. Here *Kama* is the lust but not the true love. In our *Hindu* philosophy we always burn the evil, the lust. There is a reason to do so. Lord Shiva is the creator but by default (a myth) He never shouts, He is a Man of *Mouna* but when He mean, He really means to destroy. When He opens his third hypothetical eye, universe would burn instantly. The existence of universe requires life on earth and if the Lord Shiva destroys the life, existence of whole *Brahman* ceases. We all worship Lord Shiva; I do not know worshiping Lord Brahma. Generally Hindus blame Brahma for the incest he had indulged in. There is a hidden reason for him to do so. Before Lord Brahma could commit this incestuous relationship with his own sister the Lord Shiva would have done some magic to prevent such august sin. Actually Lord Brahma is single, he had created the world and he wanted a *Purush* to enjoy this beautiful universe. Lord Brahma was in a hurry to provide the life to this world. In this confusion he would have made advances towards his own sister. From these ill advances by Lord Brahma the creator would have felt the bad urges in him; hence, from that time the Goddess Parvathi and Lord Shiva emerged as one for the true source of our life. These are all past mythological stories; let us not get obsessed on these stories. We want to convey only good to our future generations. That is how many stories were scripted with much fear and passion by late great *Sages*. In this present world there are innumerable writers who have written literatures for the young to follow in the future. Hence, let us not blame Valmiki or Vysya Maha Muni, the authors of Ramayana and Mahabaratha, respectively. If we blame these epic writers then that would allow us automatically to blame the present literatures too.

For all our ill happenings on earth, it is natural for Lord Shiva to get angry; he performs profound austerity to overcome the worldly ills by unleashing his great powers. By using this power, Lord Shiva would allow even well (good) to perish on earth. Hence, knowing the Shiva's austerity *(Thapus)* all *Devathas* worried about their life and also consequent life on earth. Many Gods and Goddesses requested Brahma to create God of love Rathi and Manamatha. The created holy pair were meant for life to continue on earth. All Gods advised this created couple to dance voluptuously in front of Lord Shiva only to bring *Thapo Banga.* So, if at all if he opens his third eye, Rathi and Manmatha would die. That is how life on earth still exists. In this melee, the pair, Rathi and Manmatha got burnt by the Lord Shiva's third eye at the expense of our life. To mark this occasion of *Thapo Banga* (time in which destruction of life was saved) we commemorate *Kama Dahana* (burning of lust), and we also remember God Kama during the festival of *Kamana Habba.*

I would like to make statement regarding our *Thrimurthy* concept; they are Brahma, Vishnu and Parameshwara. It is a parody to know that we do not praise or worship the creator, the Lord Brahma, because we are so mean that we forget the people who have helped us. We worship Lord Vishnu because he is a business deity. We all do so to earn more and more money. This is how Lord Thimmappa is richest (with due apology to the mythological story of borrowed money for His marriage?). We are scared of Lord Shiva. If we do not worship Lord Shiva or the Parameshwara, He would destroy us by opening his third eye. Hence, we all have independent selfish desires while worshiping these three Gods.

Sex is consensual and co-obligatory among the swingers. They give vivid explanations and beautiful answers for all the questions put forth by the psychologists on their behaviour. It is their personal problem; as a psychiatrist, I have to bother only for a burning issue, the safety of our future generations. This is from a particular group, a religious group that has grouped and regrouped with the help of similar social networking and also united by various technological inventions. In the swingers group, the lusty pleasure is the principle picture, which they callas true love. Particularly, in a group, love does exist, but in reality it is feigned love. The members of this group are called as the Hate Mongers. Their ideology is to hate, kill and get killed by which they would get woman and wine. This, I would like to call as a sadist love. They group themselves only to hate as 'hate mongers.' Hence, love and hate relationship have coexisted. The loss of loved ones would drive us to a state of grief. People who live in this society do go into a state of inefficiency after many acts of mass violence where dead are the mute spectators; thus, despondency increases indirectly hitting our economy hard. They are the true haters, hating values and virtues of the society. It is a disease worse than AIDS. We can manage AIDS through its prevention but not this disease of Hate, because one cannot prevent politics, religion and narrow mentality in the name of *Bhakthi*. Today's politics is growing along with appeasement, freebies and falsehood. Oneness is getting converted into "I" and this has led to 'hate disease', which is growing at a fast pace. Implosion is getting converted into explosion. Retrospection has converted into dangerous expression. People's ignorance has become innocent's death traps. Politician's petty politics has led to organised mass moral killing. The root is so strong and the bark is so thick, the diseased stem cannot be reached for an effective management and prevention. There is no known doctor for this type of disease. Each one of us who possess *Sakshi Bhava* (self-witness) is an effective 'doctor' to control such morbid disease. As a psychiatrist, the treatment for such people is not by any antipsychotics or by any antidepressants but by a cream of compassion and oil of forgiveness. It is not that easy because we have allowed this disease to grow in such a pace that our preventive measures have no known instruments or means to contain the 'hate disease'; hence, we have failed miserably at all quarters. Still, not all is that bad but mere understanding individually could prevent such diseases using a subtle drug called social justice. In our life, what we require is a mere understanding of so many religions which could prevent such horrific incidences of hate mongering and also loss of so many precious innocent lives.

COSMOS (The Orderly)

A woman in her middle age having one young child was hit badly in her temples by her husband. She presented herself to me for the management of her post-traumatic effects, secondary to her concussion of the brain. When she had come to me, she was living separately from her mother-in-law in a small town nearby along with her husband. Both of them were working as teachers. Three years after her marriage she had left home after sending a message text to her husband about her non-availability at home as she was going to her mother's place on a long holiday. The husband was angry for not discussing this mutually before she had left. She had purposefully avoided confrontation with her husband as she was sure that he would not have sent her to her mother's home instead he was interested to send her to his mother's house. This prejudiced attitude of her husband made her leave to her mother's place without informing her husband. There is reason to do so, because she hated her widowed mother-in-law for her supposed taunts. I am not a judge as to whether she is right or her widowed mother-in law-is right. After this episode, she was unable to bring her husband to me for counselling inspite of my repeated requests because he would have simply refused to come to a psychiatrist. The reason could be of his patriarchal macho or egoistic thinking. He would have also thought that what a psychiatrist could do to him. Somehow this woman who visited me wanted a change. She thought that a change in her mind is the best way to deal the mind's disturbance she had harboured. She had asked me "Dr, can you guide me by some books for my *Parivarthana*?" I was sure that she had asked this question by reading my book *Parivarthana* (the change), which was displayed on the racks in my front office. I was virtually choked by her question. I was in a dilemma to pin point a book to her on psychology. She was basically a psychology student. My literary visionary was not so much vast in recommending a book between ancient scriptures to modern personality *Guru's* books. In this moment, I failed in my task to name a book for her choice.

The change what she was talking or thinking in her young age actually began to work in my mind. After fifty-eight years of my age, with thirty years of experience in my psychiatric practice, I was ashamed for not recommending a book because whatever I had recommended she would have read beforehand. I feel a psychiatrist's role and teacher's role do go hand-in-hand-in-terms when experience and knowledge are considered. I thought the best way to deal with her problem is not by advising a book but by counselling her. I did a counselling session from psychodynamics to a little psychoanalysis and also to a little extent I tried cognitive restructuring. She was not happy by the theories put forward but she was insistent that I name a book to be read for a change in her. I thought probably my knowledge or remembrance of authors who wrote psychiatry or psychology books of the present authors are poor. Truly, I failed once again in my job of providing a good book to her. When I reached home the story of her was an enigma to me and I tried to think the true perspective of this book business. There is a reason to think in this way. Why? I have a story to explain.

A boy had come with his mother for his scholastic backwardness. My reading on cosmology was just a beginning and it had created ripples in my psyche. This was the time that this boy came to me for my counselling and treatment. What all I had read on cosmos was just passed onto this boy and I explained the modes and means of reading his subjects in a Vedanthic way. I remember telling him to make his brain empty like 'quiet' space for the subjects to go inside. It took almost an hour to counsel him. After few days of his counselling, his mother returned to me with all humbleness and she demanded me to return the fee that she had paid to me as consultation. I was curious to know the reason behind her demand. She said, "Look doctor, my son piled up all his subject books in one corner and purchased many books on cosmology by Carl Sagan." It was a rude shock to me. I felt this could be the possible reason why people are brain washed by certain religious people. This is a sort of fanatic behaviour we observe with people who are hooked to certain celebrities or with many *Dongi Swamies*. This is exactly the reason why I was scared to prescribe books of their interest when they asked me to name certain books. This brain wash is misunderstood by our youth irrespective of their education, socio-economical and religious background; they are easily brain washed by the impotent, inadequate and escapists' religious heads.

My problem about afore said couple was to make them realize their alchemy. But, the husband is not ready to lose his chemistry or bondage with his mother as he is endowed with genes of her. The wife was not ready to accept and share her chemistry because she had not shared her mother-in-law's gene. In this situation, her gene is just a witness to their frequent fights. Issues were petty from which they could not have got away easily. Her idea of meeting her mother-in-law was nauseating. Spending few minutes or spending one night with her and helping her in the kitchen would definitely drive her into hysteria. Hence, she would go choking or gasping even at the thought of her mother-in-law. It is more of a *Digbhandhana* or putting herself hypothetically in a cage. She wants liberation from all the bondages. Marriage is an eternal bondage from which no girl would try to escape as per our customs. Married positive bondage is a far cry to this couple. This negative bondage of this couple would lead to separation where leverage is a distant cry. Thus, life with them would be jerkier rather than free flow.

I had joked casually to her in my counselling session that I would lodge a complaint against her husband in the all-women's police station. This joke her husband came to know accidentally for which he became serious and came next day to my chamber with his co-brother. Both had the same complaint against their nagging (as per their husbands view) wives and they tried to prejudice me, which I refused to accept. I was not judgmental to validate their statements in the absence of their wives. They appeared shaky before they left my office as I did not budge to their complaints. When I counselled the same couple after a brief window period, I was of the opinion that they had core disparity, "Am I not helping you (wife)? Am I not looking after you (husband)?" Hours of counselling went in vain, finally my treatment failed. They had discovered beautiful treatment themselves in their next visit, Divorce.

Hence, for all problems today silence is the answer, extremes of that would be separation and the best is to live with the non-living spouse '*Yenne* (alcohol).' People applaud

Lord Buddha who had achieved *Nirvana* but today people wanted to pose like Buddha without achieving *Nirvana* or not knowing what actually *Nirvana* is all about. The reason behind some suicides is because of our social attachments or for our co-obligation with the world, which would drive us to all the known and the unknown problems. To know and to understand the art of 'no escape' we have to move along with the tide of the world.

As prerogative to 'cosmos' or 'organised', we all should make an effort to develop social cosmos or social order by an effective and on a non-discriminative interactive basis, otherwise our life would be *Naraka Yathana* (experiencing hell).

IMPOTENCY VS TELEPOTENCY ('Potency' the Common Word)

Meanings to these two words are different but both have one common denomination "potency." It is a wonderful pre-proposed concept for telepotency (telepathic knowledge based on *Vedic* knowledge), and in the meantime, imperfectly understood pre-supposed concept of impotency. As per my hypothetical philosophy, impotency is a priori, whereas telepotency is a posteriori. Reader should be meditative to that which I explain. Man always steps forward, he never step backwards. This world is too complex and full of competency, hence potencies or impotencies are the right words for an enterprising person to face this colourful world. This word impotency is being hijacked and used extensively by our politicians when the election approaches in our country. With these two directions, man keeps moving towards facing the good and the bad depending on how well he understands these two potencies. Hence, basically by this set of words with our appropriate thoughts and right actions, telepotency is hard to get. We do acquire telepotency, which would come after our lifelong difficulties faced and actually after an arduous good knowledge acquisition. From the present context, potency of a man has two clear patterns; one is polygamy potency and another is monogamy with his wife. Let me be oblivious in monogamy, and it is for the sexologists and the sociologists to discuss what they think on what I mean of my diversified ideas of potency. Who is potent? Today's common men who pay his tax regularly, do they have any potency? Do we enjoy the freedom? Do we possess constitutional rights? Do we feel that our constitutionally elected government should shower such rights on us or not? Questions keep growing as one keeps thinking deeply at a galloping pace.

For all these questions answer would be 'no' because a man with his forward momentum thinks always he is potent. This potency has been curtailed by many parameters. One such parameter is techno fear. Each forward marching man has many constraints of distrust on others. How?

- ✓ He could be a prey to a cheater.
- ✓ He could be overpowered by muzzle and money.
- ✓ There could be a possibility of threats when he is overjoyed.
- ✓ He could be a victim of emotional pranks by his superiors.
- ✓ There could be political incursions in his establishments, etc.

All these constructs associated with fear expressed or unexpressed inside a marching man towards progress have induced huge fear and wide distrust. In psychiatry, it is very well known that the cause for erectile dysfunction is the fear of the following:

- ✓ Fear of performance.
- ✓ Fear of adultery.
- ✓ Fear of alchemy.

- ✓ Fear of compatibility.
- ✓ Fear of accommodation.
- ✓ Fear of material and mind.
- ✓ Fear of celibacy, and so on so forth.

Many problems that arise in a day-to-day basis could be corrected by mutual talks and with mere acceptance in a monogamy society. However, if it still does not materialise, in some extreme cases a family counsellor, a psychologist, a psychiatrist or a sex therapist could be consulted for an effective corrective measure. However, for polygamy impotencies, the known treatment modules are sparse. Frankly, I do not know any treatment procedurals for this kind of mal-potency. Treatment could be a possibility when the following aspects are considered:

- ✓ Proper education to all.
- ✓ Correction of social extremes.
- ✓ Controlling our ever-growing population.
- ✓ Effective management of male to female ratio.
- ✓ More transparency and accountability of the government and NGO's if any.

These instruments are hard to implement because we all have one common factor that is impotency. We have seen that scared and secluded innocent men have been subjugated by the intelligent, who have allowed goons and thugs to strive in this highly competent fearful world. Hence, the potency of a person is at jeopardy. All is not that bad once again, everything is fine when we all have the right spirit and free flow attitude. Potency could be a potent when there is an understanding and acceptance. The collective effort rather than the individual effort with right approach to humanity could wipe out this social anomaly of said impotency. Is it possible to achieve this? Many who questioned were orchestrated to silence without a trace. That is why it is possible when,

- ✓ There is a collective approach.
- ✓ There is more youth participation.
- ✓ There is choosing of a right leader.
- ✓ There is discussion on future developmental issues locally.
- ✓ There is effective use of available resources.
- ✓ There is maximum effort to prevent drug abuse.

All these things can do lots to the socio-economic growth of the society. Today, politics has become dirtier and murkier, we are walking on this slush, we cannot keep simply quiet and we have to raise our potency, not literally but by our voice. Potency is directly proportional to the collective people's right involvement. I hope that the transparent politics could be a good aphrodisiac for our failing potencies in future.

Shiva's TRILOGY (The THRISHUL)

Generally, odd numbers have been considered as inauspicious by many of us. Many would feel that their car number should not possess any odd numbers. We pay lots of money to the Road Transport Office to get good even numbers for the number plates of our cars. It is for the rich to get such numbers, not for a common man like me. What difference does it make anyway? It will not do anything for me but gives something to ponder about odd numbers in Vedantha. Odd numbers under Vedanthic tradition is really auspicious. For example, Shiv's *Thrishul*, which has three projections in it, and it is like *Shaivites* who have three *Namas* on their forehead or like *Panchakshri*, who follows five ethos, which would convey enormous meanings to the vibrant society. For me, Lord Shiva's *Thrishul* reminds me the *Pindanda* (individual soul), the Heart and the *Brahmanda* (pervading souls). This is exactly what *BrahmaKumaris* preach to their followers. Their logo's depicts *Pinda* or *Athma*, which has beautiful bright spreading radiance preaching peace with Heart at the center. Lord Shiva being *Nirguna Sampanna* (beyond good) is always *Nirakara* (formless). Hence, he is formless and nameless. Center portion of *Thrishul*, which is pointing long symbolically, is meant distant vision. Hence, this *Thrishul* has *Athma* on one side and Heart on the other side, with a long pointer in the middle. The same story would address the *Nama* (marks) on Lord Thimmappa. Shiva's three *Vibhuthi* (ash) marks on *Linga* convey Lord being *Thriambaka* or the ruler of three worlds: *Akasha* (sky), Earth and *Pathala* (earth crust). When number three possess such fabulous concepts in our scriptures, why should one be scared of this odd number three. In similar fashion, we could explain the *Panchakshari* that is *Panchakshari Manthra, "Om Nama Ha Shivaya Namaha"* confining to five words. Seven depicts seven rivers, which paved for our life or gave life source in this Indus Valley and nine the good old *Nava Grahas*, who are nine brothers and sisters of our planet Earth.

Let us ignore whatever I have explained and let us meditate on a neo corporate word *'Yoga'* or a mix. Actually, the said trilogies are a bunch of lies here. For an effective true *Yoga* there must be three components, which have to be dealt comprehensively. They are reasonable enquiry, mediocre reasoning, and moderate adaptation at the practical sense. I am careful by not bringing hundred percent senses here; it is only, say fifty percent. These three mentioned constructs should always have associated qualities. Those are 1) appetite for questioning 2) thirst for knowing 3) energy for following. Therefore, we have three socio-cognizable components and three associated life qualities. To implement these things in our life, we have to have three psycho-socio instruments and those are effort, practice and patience. Imbibing such qualities by a knower would create a change in his mind functions. Thinking and working on this Trilogy, a perceptive man would instantly change. This change one could expect slowly, but for a man what change he would expect after adapting such qualities by class and means is a person of *"Prathiba* (intuitive light)*"* or a person who travels in the dark mind with a light inside. Precisely in simple words, I call this as a sixth sense.

This is what Buddha had obtained. He called this process as "Meditation." Buddha was never trained under any master; he tried to find an enlightened master but failed miserably to get one. His way of knowing was only on these three principle planes, which he got enlightened under a Banyan tree. It is time for us to know that in Buddhism we do not have *Buddha Tatwa;* whatever the *Thathwa* present under Buddhism is *Bodhi Tathwa.* Hence, a young Siddhartha changed to Buddha after enlightenment, Banyan Tree changed to speaking tree or *Bodhi* Tree. It is his three qualities of the acceptance to life, the adeptness of mind and adapting the good virtues allowed him to reach *Moksha* and not by immersing in Ganges at *Prayag* or vowing to stop eating bitter gourd permanently at Varanasi. It is the master stroke as per nine virtues, with perception Buddha could become master of *Brahman.* He did this technique not for his personal glory. There is another way of using the same technique or same instruments, which was called as Altruistic Enlightenment, the path here adopted was *Ahimsa Marg* by Gandhiji. He used this path and became *Maha Athman.* This is exactly the reason why Gandhiji was named after Mahatma. Today, a common inquisitive farmer is categorised to this group if he is destined to look after his farm with organic manure and takes care of this Mother Earth and vows to bring back her lost green glory. Any professional, a teacher, a doctor, an engineer or any man who works relentlessly under the umbrella of 'Service" with equivalent earnings is a real modern Buddha.

ADDICTION (Finding Truth on its Definition)

Any country's destiny lies with the youth. Everyone knows youths are the pillars for a strong economy in a particular state. Any future vision-oriented political candidate would admire his country's resources not by material or minerals that his country possesses but he would admire just viewing the youth power. Compulsions and obsessions have made our youth to migrate elsewhere, but still we have such a power in our society where if we tap properly the potentials of youths there are no doubts that our country would be the numero uno state in the world. There is nothing wrong in this vision and actually it is like finding the God's Particle. Yes, finding such a mystical particle by many international laboratories is still in their infancy. This research being at infant stage does not mean that scientists should lose their hopes; also, they should not allow the sponsors to close the laboratory. Everything in this world simply lies in belief, one day we might achieve one such mystic thing. There is one deterring factor to reach a top state.

This factor, which I am going to drug abuse. This substance (substance use disorders) abuse is a virtual disaster for the social unrest among developed and as well as developing nations. Drug abuse is a social mess or social anarchy for the good progress of any nation. It is unfortunate to find politicians, celebrities, bureaucrats and international sports personalities including army officials involved in such spurious drug trafficking from one place to another place. Our government agency is ill equipped to curtail or to stop such heinous activities. There are no effective legal means to punish these people. Reasons are many and are not worth discussing. For me, this Adduction is a fascinating word because when I divide this word into two, addiction appears as Add On To Dictionary. This exactly happens with multiple drug addicts. The addict is admitted to a de-addiction center and the happy parents would have shelled out huge sums of money for their wards to get cured. According to me, as a practicing psychiatrist, parents are happy when his ward is addicted to one drug, they are unhappy when their wards are addicted to multiple drugs, one more drug added to the dictionary of many drugs he abused to. When I commit addiction being a dictionary, in the world of Substance Abuse, people have created a new dictionary of coded words, as we do not find meanings to such words in our Oxford Dictionary. That is why I cry war against the Drug abuse. I mean a 'war' is to totally eradicate drugs from my Mother land but I know that it is next to impossible. At the present scenario, this war is a real issue in politics among the states bordering the neighbouring countries. There may not be terrorist's incursion but definitely drug trafficking exists. There in the border the war on terrorism is easy because our soldiers are well aware of decoding the coded words of terrorists. Candidly, we do not possess the necessary armoury to counter the drug abuse codes to decode. Our police and our army have failed to prevent the state of drug abuse, which has become a disease worse than Ebola infection. Any psychiatric or forensic textbook explains prevalence of drug abuse, its causes, biological and psychological factors pertaining to drug abuse, clinical futures of withdrawal symptoms, its diagnosis, its course and adverse effects on body and mind with the treatment, ultimately its mortality and morbidity. Addiction basically is a "Pre-supposed product of a principal pleasure constructs as a center in our neuronal system." This is a complicated chapter and with deep understanding, we could be able to dislodge the difficulties in managing the problems of addiction neuro-psychiatrically.

In our social life, we are all addicted to many pleasurable things. Apart from these outside pleasurable items, let me discuss something pleasurable inside us. It appears funny but still I feel worth mentioning. Complicity of functions of a man is beyond any body's imagination as Dr Alexis Carrel describes in his book "Man the Unknown." Leaving major collegiate departments in our body structures, I stress only on some things, which many of us fail to understand. This department is the chemistry of addiction. We never give much importance to this chapter. Examples being-addiction to eat, addiction to travel, addiction to parties, addictions to shopping, addiction to hair dye or addiction to nail polishing, forced compulsions by the temple authorities to take away our shirts before entering Sanctum Sanctorum in many orthodox temples of some states, etc. Like this, when we keep thinking on such obsessions, we have them like as in our big shopping list.

I being a psychiatrist I am bothered about our sleep pattern. Many would feel that sleep is a type of inactive state but in reality it is not so. I have many clients who say that they are unable to sleep well to a particular posture; they sleep well in another posture. What could be the reason behind good sleep for a particular posture? I consider this also as a type of obsession. What would happen inside the brain? What posture has to do for our sleep? There should be something in brain working or otherwise there is no reason for us to sleep badly. After excluding all sleeplessness under psychiatric disorders, I thought there could be some electrochemical shift from one part of the brain to another part of the brain. Could it be that it is secondary to the play of chemicals inside the brain or its wonderful subatomic condensing and non-condensing world or it could be because of some neuronal stimulation of pre-synaptic or post-synaptic receptors or is it the passing of signals in different places to and fro? The reasons behind such sleeps could be influenced by many contributing factors. In the inorganic chemistry, the elements have particular resolution and have energy to hold elements together but in the case of brain it is opposite and that is why I call addicted to sleep in a particular posture.

Reader might have experienced bad sleeps before reading my book. If not experienced, experience a bad sleep and have a thought of consulting a psychiatrist for the psychic problems this sleeplessness could have created in him. In psychiatric practice, sleep is a chief commodity. Prescription for sleeplessness made psychiatrists rich so also the psycho pharmaceutical companies. Hence, in our life, a good sleep is the hallmark of a successful and sound health. The three mind sets 1) worry, 2) hostility and 3) greed are the chief agents to disturb the smooth functioning of electrochemical neuronal function of brain. The three life instruments 1) smile, 2) trust and 3) honesty would actually improve the above said cycle, which enhances the man's sleep in any posture.

Human (The Forgotten Humanity)

I was reading an article on "To be human." What is human? Humbleness in a man is called human. In Sanskrit, same humbleness is called as Bhakthi. Our good old teachings teach us to be humble with God and to be humble with elders. If we go further, it is *Parabhakthi,* a *Yogic* concept, where the compassionate approach beyond men and women by a *Purusha* is said to have possessed pure humbleness. Hence, in medical field, it is not the drugs that help the patients but it is the treating doctor's humanitarian approaches towards such patients that conjures a cure. For me, there is a strong doubt regarding the above statement. If this statement holds good, then there should also be same reciprocation from the patient and also from the attendants or bystanders of the patient towards the treating doctor. Many a time, the doctor has been seen as a murderer or he would have been charged with certain IPC (Indian Penal Code) clause amounting to murder. He is chased, beaten and humiliated. Let me not go into details on the debate of doctor's conduct, because all professional people have the same problems. Why should there be a discussion on humans? There is a strong reason to discuss because today's world is suffering from Humanitarian reasons. Frankly speaking it is a crazy, frenzy and a religious anomaly, which does not fit into any psychiatric disorders. "C by 2" (half crack) is hard to treat and many of us fit into this group because of which we are not able to get treated until now by any psychiatrist or probably we do not have any insight to consult the mental health professionals. The condition just explained is beyond this "C by 2" problems. For my convenience sake, I call the condition just explained as "C by 3." This dreadful condition created by three sets of weird thinking groups comprising different religious fanatics. This sentence is self-explanatory (major religious groups), hence "C by 3." If we observe carefully, the defined bomb could be fitted only to a man's body. The same bomb cannot be fitted into humbleness or to a human. In general, a man with humbleness cannot attach himself to a bomb. Hence, he should not be named as humanitarian bomb, better he should be termed as Maneater. That is why humanitarian is been misquoted all over the world. He is called as "C by 3" because

- ✓ He is a perpetuator of hate among the religious lines.
- ✓ He is an inducer of fear to public.
- ✓ He is the creator of destruction by taking away the innocent lives.

Hence, he is a mean, dirty and top-grade criminal. He is a perpetuator of social anarchy, bringing anarchy in the minds of people and also anarchy to the state to govern well.

As per the evolutionist, the man is living and surviving on a dictum, "survival of the fittest." This quote is true to its core before our neo encephalon got evolved. If this dictum finds a place in today's world then this humbleness can be removed from the dictionary. The reason is that we find no human because we find only man. This man cannot be evolved to call himself as humble. Hence, man could be only an animal. Today's "C by 3" men are worst than dirty animals and the right word for them would be as *Anistas*or *Rakshashas* (evil people). Left and right wings have methods to safeguard their own suppressed people but taking away the innocent lives should not be their answers. They have many ways of expressing their views. It is true that obsessions and compulsions have made their expressions masked. A violent method to disturb harmony of society is not an answer by any fanatic group.

We have past and present existentialist who by their philosophy convey nihilism being the master of one's success. This alienisms' attitude is too painful for the man to accept. It is hard to digest the pain the man experiences from this sort of anarchists mind set. In our country, especially difficulties have been well taken care by the parents till teenage. All the problems start when they reach their adulthood. We have excelled in eradicating small pox and polio from our country. We are not able to eradicate 'difficulties.' Because we failed to adopt a mechanism wherein we have failed to inoculate little pain to our children, which would bring peacefulness in their life by the adaptations for the ever-growing difficulties they face later on. Hence, for an ordinary man, this world is 'difficulty' and always looks problematic. In this realistic and virtual world, man by de facto does not want to face problems in their life. Facing problems or not facing the problems, the humbleness or the humanity is parting away far and far or widening more and more. Thus what remained here in this world is only a man, not human. This is what exactly happens with "C by 3" people who wanted to live in a problem-free world up, a mystique world of woman and wine after taking away the innocent lives here. This is a simple way of escaping by a man from this world comprising with full of difficulties and lots of problems. Many suicides we observe today apart from major psychiatric disorders fall to the group of escapism. Difference would be, one is brainwash and another is self-wash. It is better in our life that if we wash our dirty self by *Prathiba* or a ray of light. The said light is nothing but knowledge, on the other hand, it allows self to look in to the path of realisation. This realisation with *Samyama* (patience) would prevent bomb explosion in future, hence the self-explosion.

ARITHMETIC AND DOGMATIC (The Job Compared to Numbers)

People learn and get moulded by their simple observations. These repeated observations in this world would increase their moulding capacity by three-folds of their learning capacity. This could be a possibility with a keen observer who practices the art of observation. I have the opportunity for many such observations in this world. I am thankful to be born in this Mother Earth and that is why I am *Purushothama* (superior being) because of the simple reason that Mother Earth has endowed me the brain (*Chittha*) by default. This *Chittha* of mine taught me how to observe the events in this Mother Earth. I consider this offer by my Mother Earth as a gift. I cannot make a brain like mine artificially to sell or to market in the malls. Probably this could be a possibility in near future as we are manufacturing intelligent robots matching almost humans. It is a basic necessity on a day-to-day basis to have a heightened awakening to observe and learn the good ones in this fast environmental interaction. I being a psychiatrist, I could be prejudiced after observing others where I would format a text in my mind software falsely. I am sure this text of mine on any person would not hold the truth because another person's view on the same person could be different. Hence, the text folders in our brain are always relative. My friends too are not spared for my own prejudiced text scriptures on them. One such friend is a practicing doctor who shifted present professionalism to original family agricultural practices. Hence, given the chance I call him as a Plant Doctor. Many friends of his including me were of the opinion that he was very meticulous in his duties, he never opted for a change, he never budged to any kind of advices from his friends and also he was confined to his own hard logics. This attitude of his drew lots of criticism from many of his friends and probably also from his family members too. Because of this nature, he kept to himself from many of his friends and also from his own family members. He was labeled as Dogmatic. This title of him bothered me and I wanted to know the Dogmatic against the Arithmetic because of his meticulous nature or behaviour. I worked on this and found something amazing, which I want to share with the readers.

According to my understanding this Matic and Metic meant *Yanthric* (robotic). When I go little deeper inside this Matic, what I found was 'automatic.' Automatic behaviour what we see today in this competitive world of technological progress has converted humans to Robots. Technically speaking, man is not a robot because a robot is there for a specific function whereas a man's mind exists for multiple functions. Robots function for a product, which reaps material, whereas human has no such ambitions and he is here on earth for only to serve and to earn material, to lead a good life. Robot has value for material; man is valued for his panacea. My hypothesis is that this Metic is limited to a framework or structure when worked with in this framework would deliver a fruit. Let us not pave ourselves into confusions. At this context, 'fruit' means meaning to our life process. The end product of this kind of fruit should have some meaning or could be a useful fruit for another person to use. This analogy would narrate the meaning of *Paraa* (altruistic) as the fruit reaped by a tree is not for the same tree to eat. The same explanation could be given to the *Arth* in Sanskrit. Hence, today our in numerous numerical problems are because of this *Arth-Metic* (robotic to the numerical). We pay hefty money to RTO (Road Transport Office) for allotting an even number to our vehicles. We are scared of odd numbers. There are instances of losing our lives for adding, subtraction and multiplications. This is what I call the parody, because we never divide the numerical, if a person divides his personal possession this personal possessions would get diluted.

I remember one of my friends calling his father "You bastard" for the simple reason that until his father death his father never divided his wealth between two of his sons. Likewise, in our life journey, we keep hearing these things and seeing many such things. According to me, this is one such example as how Sanskrit literature extended its potential tentacles to English, not only to English literature, for that matter to many different literatures like in German literature, Russian literature, Greek literature, Hebrew literature, etc. In our ancient mythological scriptures, we have many metaphorical terms against many verbs and nouns and in that there is one mythological God Lord Narayana who falls to this category. Hence, He is worth narrating. My friend's granny had developed compulsion to touch a dog as she would see Lord Narayana inside the dog. In this way, in our Hindu philosophy, dog and God has been connected since ages. In what way is Lord Narayana connected to dog is a million dollar question for a moderate rationalist? There is an interesting story behind these million dollars. *Nara* (body) is actually a *Purush* when gone on a *Yana* (travel) or who go out on a vacation has been called as *Nara-Yana*. While *Purush* (owner of the dog) was on vacation, his home should be guarded. A human guard is not trustworthy when compared to the dog, which takes care as a guard for its master's home. Thus, a dog could give its utmost care through its *Niste* (submitting cent percent duty to its master). The dog guards from the thefts and from the burglary by its relentless duty to its master. Hence, we always remember Lord Narayana when we are out from our homes on vacations. Now, this *Niste* (duty) of this dog is almost automatic or robotic hence the word Dogmatic. This interpretation is mine own hypothetical presumption. The dog does not heed or listen to anyone and would attack any person other than its master. The same analogy holds good for my friend to whom I was referring to. His submission to his duty is so strong that he would not have listened to anybody. In our life, Arithmetic and Dogmatic both have wonderful meanings, but the pain of knowing both and the art of mixing both would always provide food for our thoughts. Automatic nature of a person does not help the life unless it has some meaning to ever facing psycho-social problems, which are totally different from numerical problems (additions and multiplications) to which we always get engaged with. Intelligent quotient of a hundred and sixty-two does not have the same propensity to little social quotient or life quotient. Converting IQ (intelligent quotient) to EQ (emotional quotient) has lots of meaning in our life. In the process of achieving this 'U' turn is an ordeal task the man could face (if he is intends to have a 'U' turn by the way). The effort and persuasion from a man could bring the change to an ever smiling flower of living beings. And also it would allow for us to experience a harmonious mystic fragrant social aroma.

MY DOUBLE FIST FOREHAND SHOT (A Change Would Mean More)

Dear readers kindly follow my statement "Young change to old but old would not change to young." This is true as long as our body is concerned, but same does not hold well for our mind because our old politicians still aspire to become a prime minister. I have made my point clear in my earlier book (Parivarthana—the change) regarding how does a young doctor think on an old doctor. Briefly, our skeleto-muscular system can be compared to a 'Chasis (metallic frame work)' of a car. The tensile capacity of the 'Chasis' of a vehicle cannot revert back as age advances of this vehicle but we humans can revert back the same with vigour not by muscular power but by our intuitive mind power. This is exactly the reason why politicians aged eighty to ninety years yearn for the post of prime ministerialship. For our politicians, there is no retirement age. As I grew older, my fascio-skeleto-musular system fails to come under my control. Even though my age is fifty-eight years, I was as enthusiastic as any 40-year old tennis player when my tennis playing techniques are considered. My mind was not listening to my body. Ultimately, it is the stress to my body system which takes up my skeleto-muscular toll, but to tell the truth, playing tennis relieved my stress successfully. When I met an orthopedician for my problem, he had encouraged me to take rest and even asked me to stop playing tennis for some period. I did not listen to him because playing is the only spirit (not alcohol) for me to relieve my stress. While playing, I developed right hand ring finger bursitis, which led to trigger finger probably due to my bad grip techniques. I developed severe tendinitis with fibro-myositis on my right wrist. My single-handed forehand shots were like a nightmare to me. Playing big shots on the court would lead to lot of pain in my right wrist. I decided to change my playing techniques or otherwise not play tennis, which would have left toxic thoughts in my mind. Playing sports is a good de toxic agent. I would advise the readers to play and to have minimum exercise to keep ourselves little younger. Hence, changing my style of playing forehand shot was a basic necessity.

One woman who had visited me for her writer's cramp enquired me about her practicing left hand writing. I had encouraged her to practice so. After several months of practice, she could write fluently with her left hand. She could improve on this after encouragements given by me to her in my counselling sessions. She had improved her writing skills after her rigorous practice. With this change in her writing practice she had passed her competitive examination with top marks. This story she had expressed in a TV show *"Kannadada Kotyadi Pathi"* when she had occupied the hot seat. I came to know her submission from my friends. After watching her in the re-telecast program, she became an instant model for me. After I listened to her story, I tried playing tennis left handed. With continuous practice, I could pick up left hand tennis fairly well but I became master in my tennis club with transformed double fist fore hand shot. My tennis mates used to call me as Miss Bartholi for my style of playing. One day. I began to think what actually worked for this different technique of my play. When I came to know the dynamics of physiology I was really thrilled. I am not a mechanical professor or sports specialist. My observations tell me that after my life-saving surgery, my abdomen was not in the center but actually it moved to left lower quadrant. When I realised my force on double fist fore hand behind the ball was naturally more, I could feel the ball leaving my racquet at a good speed. This speed that I could acquire is probably because of two reasons. The basic pivoting system I learnt from my left toe is one reason and next reason could be the extra 10 kg abdomen I got after the surgery and that extra 10 kg weight (twenty years ago I underwent AP resection with permanent colostomy for adenoid carcinoma rectum, as days passed, the fat, pushed peritoneum with probable hernia of small intestines. Thinned out muscles and enlarged colon near and around my stoma increased local part into extra ten kg. I do not know how long my present abdominal condition allows me to play tennis) behind the tennis ball was generating more power. Both were blessing in disguise to play such shots without injuring my right wrist and palm. Frankly, I was pleased to the wonders of such transformation in me. As each days passed with perfectness I began searching for various other reasons. I have explained few of them in earlier concepts. Hence, in our life if are awake, if we are more aware, if we are always observing and if we are able to keep on answering the observations we have made would allow us to move towards perfection. While reaching perfection there could be hurdles, fine accepting and finding meanings for these hurdles takes us to the limited liberations. When I scanned Bruce Lee's quote, what he quoted come closer to my statement, which I had explained before, states as "Every effort from heart and mind should be there in us to move forward with hopes and success. We may reach or might not reach; when reached, we find the bliss, when we do not reach, we find the reason. The reasons found would take us to the Himalayas; bliss takes us to *Manasa Sarovar*." Always new things in our life would land us in many problems but these problems are minimal when compared to the problems we encounter without an attempt of such problems in our life. My new technique lands me into burning plantar pad of my left great toe but this is nothing when compared to my wrist problem. Hence, playing with scissor like footsteps I developed little LS (lumbar sacral) strain. I did not bother to this strain because I could prevent my wrist injury from getting worse. After all, a human is mere mass of bones and flesh with motion, inertia and velocity. The three aspects 1) good racquet, 2) fine shoes and 3) right grip are the pre-requisites for an injury-free play, so also in our life too 1) a good inquisitiveness, 2) a fine thinking and 3) the right attitude would allow us to become more human. The right court to play and the right society to live are also the true *Manthras* for the right moves to our perfection. We are prone to injuries while playing so also while overcoming many hurdles in this world. Hence, man should find the ways to minimise injuries while playing and in similar fashion he should also try to minimise despondency in this ever interactive problem riddled world.

LANGUAGE (To Remember the Philosopher)

In our psycho-socio interactive life, language is most valued when compared to the mind and matter. The language is directly linked to our thinking. Hence, sometime this language could construct or destroy, which I have already mentioned in my first book Parivarthana (the change). Because of this innate property of humans, people keep their art of language in their lockers and bring out whenever it is necessary against the material and money. Hence, good talking or good language has found no place in the present dictionary. To whatever the reader would think of me, I am straight forward to make my point clear, that is "We are thieves." The culprit is being our genes. This gene what we possess today does not honestly belong to us and also it is not the property of this present world. It is true that there are few who have excellent quality of language expression and others or majority of us have no such ability. We stole this language from the philosophers who had lived two thousand five hundred years ago. Our language stands testimony to the great work done by these forgotten philosophers. This present 'language' has not come easily and also it is not new, it had come through bygone philosopher's philosophical inquires. These inquiries were screened and refined in the court of generational consciousness with 1) discrimination, 2) deliberations and 3) argumentations.

Such evolved languages have been printed on our genes in due course of generations and in turn we are ready forwarding these refined languages to our progenies. This is also an important part in our evolution.

From the erstwhile philosophers' with their great struggle, the evolved and refined language has been coded in our genes and presently the same would get decoded in our consciousness. This is how as generations passed, on this day, we have an intelligent man evolved with super Neo Encephalon. Presently the evolved new brain has the capacity to store innumerable codes and it gets decoded whenever we would ask for. Probably the environment plays a Uno role in making man a challenge in the court of fast and furious world wherein we all play dangerous games. Environmental cues certainly throw man dizzy or spinning to find a suitable comfort zone in this mundane. For this entire phenomenon, the learnt language is a most important weapon. Today's intelligence is gauged by different parameters like arithmetic quotient, social quotients, life quotients and emotional quotients. Hence, mind is not a proprietor to single quotient. In the process of human evaluation as peoples brain and intelligence grew leaps and bounds a group of philosophical thinkers evolved. Their arguments is that (if I want to explain concisely), in the past human life had lacked meanings hence man wandered haphazardly and helplessly to find a meaning. In other words, man's existence in the past was purposeless. Today's man welcomes Gods but never think of any philosopher or for that matter a scientist. So, God is Omniscient where his mind is full of innocence and ignorance, He does not fit into any form of intelligence or knowledge but still we worship Him. In this scenario, we forget worshiping people who possess knowledge or who are enlightened masters. This could have been a possible reason for the Lord Buddha to leave our country.

Imagine if a nurse or mother is not there for a child who has not yet opened his or her eyes. Child is always scared and gets more scared as outside signals keeps piercing this mass of life. When this happens, there would have been only chaos in the child's mind. This is exactly the reason why existentialists argued, "When a growing child keeps finding the reasons for its chaotic mind, as the child grows to older and older there could be a tendency for the growing man to be more humane." Hence, while in the aura of not finding meanings by growing man, instead he experiences the mirage of money and material and thus the despondency and depression in him. Many die like ants and flies but large chunk of men find meaning and they would lead meaningful life later. It is really a possibility because free will has no role and even if it is there it is within the ambit of psycho-social framework. For a man, this world is always full of discomfort zones. It is the momentum and dynamism of him which would require in finding the comforts in these discomfort zones. As a psychiatrist, we tend to prescribe depot shots to chronic schizophrenics. Similarly, creator is so compassionate that he had injected depot hormones lasting for one hundred years in man. It is not the psychiatrist who regulates these depot hormones but an invisible part of our body, the self or the soul, who is only the chief agent, which can regulate such depot hormones.

In our evolutionary process, animals are devoid of language because of their poorly developed brain system but God has endowed them with good communications system by which they emotionally well connected with their own species and also with other species including humans. Animals are ferocious only to look at, ferocious in its mind to live and survive. The man is appeasing and appears harmless but in reality his mind is most ferocious than animals. For animals, man never looks like a hunter but he appears like a Yama (God of Death). Animals are very sensitive with their innate sixth sense. They could sense calamities better than we. Today the same sixth sense is been used by these animals to escape from dirty men. Animals cannot provide all answers for man's greed. Animals are contended with their limited language and communication, but not man. Man possess many types of armoury, one of them is their dirty mouth from which they escape from all the ills they commit. If we go into the depth of our language and carefully try to analyse, the language as a cognitive agent would ascertain many ills with a good text of words and exist as folders in our brain. These folders present in mind are important for our well-being when a problem that would arise in the environment only to safeguards oneself from the disturbances this problem could produce. The ill occasionally does happen in our society. When these ills would take place in the society or we tend to observe? For example, the politician's speech, will his speech be converted into deeds? The language of a conman or pseudo-saints *Pravachanas*, listening to him make his followers better? The skilled business man's talking techniques, would it help the buyer by purchasing his product? The cheaters who articulate their language to cheat would help common man's savings? The psychopath who controls men with his dubious jugglery of words would make psychopath better? The manipulator manipulating our portfolios, etc. would make a man philanthropic? Generally, I know a peasant who would meet his ends daily always uses his language properly. Hence, the beauty of *Mouna,* as refined language was been followed and adopted by Lord Buddha. This is exactly the reason why Lord Buddha never spoke; he spent two-third of his lifetime with utmost silence. He was the master of "No language." He never would have written the scriptures and spoken on life but what scriptures we find today like *Mahayana* and *Hinayana* are the works of his disciples like Nagarjuna (Great South Indian King). Lord Buddha was a real acceptor, a great perceptive and a remarkable conceiver. Viewing these antimonies, man fails to answer a simple question "Is language a connector or a destroyer?" Seventeenth century philosophers tried to find answers through their critical nature of pure reasoning which led to Parivarthana (a change) of languages. For dynamic life, the language is a medium. One such medium is Hindi, which south Indian people are reluctant to learn. Could any person be able to connect this India where so many languages exist? Truly this is a billion dollar question.

Criticism is previewed as demoralising and demonising. Criticism draws argumentations and corrections of the languages. Criticism would allow refining and clarifications of the deeds. Criticism is a healthy approach for transcendence of man to the super human. Criticism could help one's thoughts and feelings for their integration. Criticising me would mean nothing; honestly, criticise me to strengthen the answers to the pervading worldly apathy and lack of excitement.

To conclude, it is appalling to find that world has been falling apart:

- ✓ by religious lines
- ✓ by ethnical lines
- ✓ on border issues
- ✓ by economical standards
- ✓ frequent changing policies of various countries
- ✓ by military might
- ✓ from mineral resources
- ✓ by political indifferences
- ✓ from many psychosocial parameters of individuals and also on other in numerable unseen and unfelt reasons, which necessitates a urgent call on each individual to bring out an virtuous instrument from his own consciousness to apply in the society for bringing a change in the worldly inevitable regression to the practical progression at all spheres in order to generate minimum solace (in Kannada *Nemmadi).*